Praise for
FIND A WAY

"I've covered sports for 40 years, half of them with ESPN, the NFL for more than a quarter-century, and Merril Hoge first got my attention when he was a player. Actually, Merril demanded my attention because he was one of those truth-is-better-than fiction stories. There's an old adage that in every one of us, there is a good book. In Merril Hoge's story, there is a great book and it is FIND A WAY. Merril's story is a unique profile of courage and inspiration, written in the only manner my friend and colleague knows how to tell a story—head-on—with transparency and with a heart that is immeasurable. I've learned plenty of football from Merril; I have learned more about life in FIND A WAY."

—Chris Mortensen, senior NFL analyst & reporter, ESPN

"In this book, Merril Hoge shows the same drive and determination that were his trademarks as an NFL player. In his life today as a broadcaster and businessman, Merril exudes enthusiasm, energy, and tenacity. No matter what the obstacle or the goal, he ALWAYS finds a way...and you will find this an inspirational read!"

—Hannah Storm, ESPN anchor, president of the Hannah Storm Foundation and Brainstormin Productions

"I had the pleasure of being one of Merril's coaches at Idaho State and with the Pittsburgh Steelers. On and off the field Merril was always determined to "find a way." After reading this book, I'm confident you will be just as motivated and determined as he has always been. It's a testimonial to overcoming the odds no matter what the circumstances."

—Marvin Lewis, head coach, Cincinnati Bengals

"Merril and I have been more than teammates, we have been like brothers! I have seen him find his way to live his dream of playing in the NFL, and I have seen him find his way to live as he fought through head trauma that ended his career and cancer that threatened his life! After reading his book I felt that magic that lies within me like he found in himself and those that read it will find it as well."

—Bubby Brister, NFL QB for the Steelers, Broncos, Jets, and Eagles

"As a former teammate and personal friend I have always admired Merril Hoge, and now I know why. Merril Hoge embodies a life force that compels man to higher levels of achievement. He is a testament to the heart, will, and determination of the human spirit. And now, he peels back the layers of his own life to generously help others to find their own way to emerge triumphant through life's inevitable adversities."

—Solomon Wilcots, CBS Sports/NFL Network
game analyst and reporter

"From Highland High School, to the Pittsburgh Steelers, to ESPN, to beating cancer, Merril Hoge has always been able to "find a way" to beat the odds. Merril is not only an inspiration, but offers practical life lessons that have enabled him to be a self-made success story."

—Dirk Koetter, offensive coordinator, Jacksonville Jaguars

"Merril and I have been connected long before our days as analysts on ESPN. In college we battled against one another, me as an Idaho Vandal and Merril as an Idaho State Bengal. I've always had great respect for Merril as a player, analyst, and colleague. As I've spent time reading Merril's amazing story, I am reminded of the power of the human spirit. Merril's courage and positive attitude are truly inspiring and I am proud to call him my friend. As you read this incredible story of perseverance do yourself a favor…grab a pen and take notes, that's what I did! Thanks Merril, for sharing your journey!"

—Mark Schlereth, sports analyst and commentator

"Merril inspires me by his will, strength, and relentless passion for life and people. He has been a motivational force for me."

—Jay Rothman, television producer, ESPN

FIND A WAY

THREE WORDS THAT CHANGED MY LIFE

MERRIL HOGE

WITH

BRENT COLE

FOREWORD BY RON JAWORSKI

CENTER STREET

New York   Boston   Nashville

Center Street
Hachette Book Group
237 Park Avenue
New York, NY 10017

www.centerstreet.com

Center Street is a division of Hachette Book Group, Inc.
The Center Street name and logo are trademarks of Hachette Book Group, Inc.

Printed in the United States of America

First Edition: September 2010
10   9   8   7   6   5   4   3   2   1

Library of Congress Cataloging-in-Publication Data

Hoge, Merril.
    Find a way : three words that changed my life / Merril Hoge with Brent Cole.
        p. cm.
    ISBN 978-1-59995-305-2
  1. Hoge, Merril.   2. Football players—United States—Biography.
3. Sportscasters—United States—Biography.   4. Cancer—Patients.
I. Cole, Brent.   II. Cole, Brent.   III. Title.

GV939.M29H64 2010
796.332092—dc22
[B]
                                                        2010020582

There is no way I could take all the credit for the victories I have enjoyed or the challenges I have overcome. My life has been a product of so many great people who have inspired me and challenged me to find a way. This book is dedicated to every one of them.

It is also dedicated to you, my reader. I would not have written this book if I were not rooting for you to find a way to your own victories. I know you can.

Contents

Acknowledgments

I owe a debt of gratitude to many people who helped me pave the path I've traveled down:

- Chuck Noll and Walter Payton, for having the greatest impact on me both personally and professionally
- The Steelers organization and specifically the Rooney family, for their unwavering support and consistency
- The Bears organization and the Bears fans, for welcoming me with open arms—it still hurts that I could not play for them longer
- Great coaches like Bill Cowher, for being like an older brother to me, my college coach Jim Koetter, and my high school coach Dirk Koetter, for helping mold me as a teenager
- My teammates, for being like family to me—I still miss playing with all of them
- Bubby Brister, my one teammate who stood out above the rest, for his unselfishness and incredible generosity to me

ACKNOWLEDGMENTS

- ESPN, for giving me a chance when I was second-guessing myself, for standing by me as I battled cancer, and for giving me the opportunity to work with so many great people every day
- Myron Cope and Bill Hillgrove, for putting up with an inexperienced, concussed former player early in my broadcasting career
- My brother Marty, for being my greatest fan—I am equally proud of him
- Ron "Jaws" Jaworski, for being one of my dearest friends and for teaching me so much about football
- Jeff Spadafore, my high school buddy and best friend, for keeping laughter in my life
- The Steeler Nation, whom I am constantly in awe of, for making me feel as if I'm still playing today
- WDVE, for helping me discover my love of broadcasting
- The Leukemia & Lymphoma Society and Genentech, for all the amazing work they do to find a cure for cancer
- The Highmark Caring Place and Charlie LaVallee, for recognizing a great need in those who suffer the loss of a loved one—they are a sanctuary for so many children and their families
- Dr. Joe Maroon and Dr. Mark Lovell for their expert care during my head traumas
- Dr. James Bradley, Dr. Richard Rydze, Dr. Anthony Yates, and Dr. Stan Marks, and my nurses, Becky and Lois, for being my family throughout my cancer treatment

- To all who care for cancer patients; they are so often a major catalyst for beating the disease
- My mom and dad, whom I will always honor
- Toni, for being an amazing mother to Kori and Beau

My daughter, Kori, and my son, Beau, for being two of the most amazing people I have ever met in my life and for giving me the blessing of sharing life with them—I want them to always know I love them with all I am.

Foreword

Over my seventeen-year career in the NFL, I played with and against some of the greatest athletes of all time. Merlin Olsen, John Hadl, Jack Snow, Jerry Sisemore, Bill Bergey, Dan Marino, and Derrick Thomas were my teammates. Dick Butkus, Randy White, Lawrence Taylor, Joe Montana, and Terry Bradshaw were worthy opponents. Observing and sharing the field with such giants of the game helped me develop a profile for what it takes to succeed in the brutal business of professional football. I could fill several pages of this book with the lessons I've learned from them. However, no player has taught me more than my dear friend Merril Hoge. As you read further in this book, you will see exactly what I mean.

As a player, Merril's career teaches us that it is possible to overcome even the greatest challenges inside and outside our control. Merril believed in himself and his resourcefulness was his greatest resource. That is all that mattered in the long run. He simply found a way to succeed, to overcome adversity, and to continually improve time and time again. I was always looking for that type of guy when I played. I knew he would be a difference-maker.

As a person, Merril stands out from the crowd. When we work together on any number of ESPN shows, I always know I better be prepared because he always is. But what makes him so rare is that it is possible to totally disagree with him and still maintain mutual respect and enjoyment. Everyone knows that number thirty-three still believes in prehistoric football. You run the ball. I believe in the passing game. You throw to score and run to win. Our philosophical differences add flare to our conversations but we always have a blast together.

However, what stands out the most is Merril's character. I have never been associated with someone who has more. I love Hogee for his ability to be a tempo and standard setter. He leads by example.

I think about when he and I were working the NFL draft together while he was going through intense chemotherapy. As we neared the end of the live, two-day coverage, I could see that he was fading. I told him to wrap it up and go get some rest. I would finish the last couple hours.

How wrong I was.

He looked at me like I'd slapped him in the face and said, "I will finish this." Then he stayed until the very end. He even did the post-draft wrap up before getting the rest he deserved more than any of us.

If I've learned anything about Merril Hoge, I've learned that he knows how to find a way. In my opinion, there is no one more qualified to write this book. I know his words and example will make you a bigger, better, and stronger person, just as they have for me.

Ron "Jaws" Jaworski

FIND A WAY

You Pave Your Path as You Go

I was driving on a Kentucky highway nine years after my NFL career ended when a van going fifty miles per hour broadsided me. The impact of the accident tore the labrum in my left shoulder, which required surgery. The procedure and rehabilitation went fine, but several months later, when I ducked my head into the shower, I felt a sharp pain in my back.

Working through injuries is commonplace in the world of football, so I treated this situation no differently than I had throughout my career. I sought the quickest and best way to get better. During a follow-up appointment for my shoulder, I mentioned the back pain to the Steelers' team physician, Dr. James Bradley, who had remained my doctor after my career. He ran a few tests. The results concerned him.

"Right now one plus one equals three," he said. "There's no clear problem with your neck or back, but I need to figure out what the other factor is."

Three hours into what was supposed to be a routine, half-hour checkup, Dr. Bradley sent me to get an MRI. I was already late for another obligation, so after climbing out of the booth, I hopped in my car and sped off. I wasn't halfway there when Dr. Bradley's number appeared on my cell phone.

"I gotta have you come back," he said. "This can't wait."

Irritated by the inconvenience, I flipped an illegal U-turn and returned to his office. There he explained that he arranged an appointment with a specialist the following morning. It still didn't register with me that all of this was about much more than a pulled muscle or pinched nerve.

I went to see the specialist the next morning. As I pulled into the parking lot, I read a sign on the building: Hillman Cancer Institute. *Odd place for a back specialist's office,* I said to myself.

I rode the elevator to the right floor, walked around a corner, and opened the office door. I then walked into a waiting room full of people I didn't expect to see. All around the room were patients with bald heads or wearing scarves. I finally began to realize what was happening. I approached the counter and the receptionist told me they'd been expecting me. She led me to an observation room.

A few minutes later, four white coats entered, and a Dr. Marks introduced himself. He and three others threw my back scans on the wall and muttered among themselves.

I overheard one doctor say, "Looks like...," but I didn't understand the word that came next.

"Looks like what?" I asked.

Dr. Marks turned and looked at me. "Mr. Hoge...it looks like cancer."

I sat silent, motionless, staring at the doctor. I felt darkness, as if every light went out inside my body. I was empty. Doubtful. Fearful.

Cancer.

For a brief moment I thought about the irony of my emotions. Throughout my college and pro career I was honored for being a tough guy...Iron Man of the Year...All Madden Team...didn't miss a game in eleven years...played with every injury known to man: broken foot, ribs, fingers, and hand, separated shoulder, torn groin, fractured hip and tibia, concussion, etc. And yet, hearing the word *cancer* spoken in the same breath as my name made me forget everything. I shrank into uncertainty. I wanted back every injury I had ever suffered simultaneously in order to take away this battle.

I knew I was not merely staring into the fierce eyes of great linebackers like Lawrence Taylor, Mike Singletary, and Derrick Thomas. I was staring into the face of death.

Once I could speak, I asked every question I could think of. I had the doctors walk me through various scenarios, trying to reason my way out of the sentence I'd just received.

The lab needed several days to collect the official results and determine the next step. I left Pittsburgh without definitive answers and drove back to my home in Kentucky. The dark, four-hour drive was fogged with ambiguity. I reflected on my life: regrets...joys...accomplishments. The pride I felt for being a good father stood out.

If there is one thing I love more than playing football or talking about it on ESPN, it's being a dad. I had a dad who worked hard to provide for us but did little else to help my three brothers and me become men. I vowed to change that legacy when I was blessed with kids. And I had.

Now, driving on that dark road home with thoughts of the cancer inside me, all I wanted was more time. More time to love them, teach them, and prepare them for an abundant life. I lost my mom in college and then witnessed the suffering it caused my younger brothers. As I began to relive those feelings, I imagined my children and me jumping on our trampoline out back the way we always did.

Who would be there to jump with them if I was gone? Who would help them and protect them in times of need?

From the deepest part of my soul, I began sobbing like a baby.

My wife, Toni, and I sat alone that night and talked. We would wait on telling our children, Kori and Beau, until the biopsy results came back. Explaining the news to them would be heart-wrenching, and we wanted to be 100 percent sure this was happening before we did it.

Weeks earlier we had planned a family vacation to our cabin in Idaho. The trip was only days away now, and we wondered if we should still go or stay home and await the news. After much deliberation we kept our plans, hoping deep down if we got away we might also escape the disease.

Our remote spot in Idaho is pristine. Lit by a million stars, the nights often feature the towering silhouette of a moose gliding by the cabin and disappearing into the black lake. There I can withdraw from the grind. On this visit, I hoped I would more than ever.

The hope didn't last long.

The phone rang one day into the trip, Valentine's Day, 2003. I was alone upstairs. It was Dr. Marks, the oncologist. He was calling with the results of the biopsy. I was done with the wondering and worrying. I wanted to *know* something. My heart raced as I picked up the phone. I took a deep breath. Said hello. Then listened.

"It's cancer, Merril—non-Hodgkin's lymphoma. You have a two- to three-pound tumor in your back the size of a small football."

I heard all he explained next—the time line...the chemotherapy...the hair loss. But I had stopped thinking of myself.

One question dominated my mind: what would this mean for Kori and Beau?

They needed to know right away. I closed my eyes and exhaled. I had to unpack reality without sugarcoating the situation or scarring their young minds. Talking with them was never a problem. We talked about everything. But sharing this news would be torture. I had to help them understand why their daddy was going to be a little different than he normally was, why I was going to start being tired and sick a lot, and, after a few more weeks, bald. I despised the task.

As the sun descended behind the lake and calm woods, the

four of us sat together in the great room. I sat forward in my leather chair, and as I looked into their innocent faces, I could barely find the words to speak.

"Things are going to be a little different over the next few weeks," I explained. "Daddy is going to be sick and will probably lose some weight. I'm also going to be tired and have to lay down on the couch a lot more than you're used to seeing me lay down."

Beau was seven, and as I pressed through my speech, he fumbled with his toys on the floor. Kori was nine, and her wide blue eyes remained glued to mine. She could sense this was more than her daddy having a cold.

Then I said it.

"Daddy has something called cancer...and in a couple weeks I will start to look different because the medicine I have to take is probably going to make all my hair fall out."

There was silence when I finished speaking. I think it was more difficult for me to tell them than for them to hear it. I bowed my head and stared at the floor. A lot had changed in a few short days.

I looked up after an emotional pause. What I saw was the catalyst for my triumph over an unjust, unforgiving killer.

Kori, my blond-haired, blue-eyed angel, jumped from the couch and ran to my chair. She threw her dainty arms around me and stretched up to whisper something in my ear.

"Daddy, you're just gonna have to find a way."

It floored me.

Since she was old enough to understand, I'd been encouraging her to find her own way through life's challenges. Now this extraordinarily wise child was guiding me. Now my little angel echoed the advice back to me, and it filled my body with a fire that would not quit.

I *would* find a way, *no matter what* it took.

I descended those stairs minutes earlier lugging an enormous burden. My spirit was hollow. I was crawling toward death. Dr. Marks had explained my treatment options but offered no guarantees. I had already begun considering how to best savor my last few months. Kori's words rescued me from that defeatist mind-set. She reminded me of a lifelong philosophy I had forgotten amidst the swirl of emotions.

I looked in her eyes and saw her strength—my strength. Blood rushed through my body and I sat up straight and strong, holding Kori close to me.

In that moment, I was committed to fight the beast.

I said nothing aloud but spoke volumes in my spirit. *I might go bald,* I asserted to myself, *but feeling tired and negative is not an option. Getting sick is not an option. And dying is definitely not an option.*

I will *find a way through this.*

Life quickly moved on when seven-year old Beau blurted, "Dad, can we go to Wal-Mart?"

I suppose neither of us knew how brutal the battle would be.

His words were an innocent reminder of how, in a million

years, he never imagined that life with Mom, Dad, and Sister would be any different.

I would make sure he was right.

I sat alone in a dim room one week later. The soft chairs, scenic portraits, and baby-blue uniforms are a thoughtful but futile respite in a chemotherapy clinic. Especially when someone dressed in a hazmat suit enters the room cradling a large red-liquid-filled syringe.

Many cancer patients call Adriamycin "Red Death." The nickname comes from its bloody color and what it's capable of. It is one of the most potent of all chemotherapy treatments.

I will never forget that scene. I squinted, breathing slowly through my nose while nurse Becky prepared a vein. In less than a minute she pushed the poison into my forearm. She then confessed there was always a difference in the mind-set of those who beat the disease.

"If you want to survive," she calmly asserted, "the majority of it is up to you now."

The chemicals exploded through my entire body, attacking and destroying. A burning sensation was everywhere, tangibly pulsing my veins. The nurses served me ice chips to keep the thin lining of my mouth from breaking out in sores. I remained statue-like in the soft recliner—collected yet fully aware my insides were being eaten away.

While Red Death tore through my body, I was given fluids through another IV. My bladder was stretched to capacity within minutes. I slid off my chair and stood delicately.

"Make sure you flush twice," the nurse interjected.

Embarrassed, I confessed I just really had to go.

"I know," she said. "And what I just put into you was poison—one hundred percent. It will come out of you at about eighty percent potency. If any of it sits in the toilet, it will eat through the porcelain."

I didn't believe her, but I staggered into the bathroom and did my business with those words in mind. I looked into the bowl and my heart sank. There was a pool of liquid as red as what I saw in the syringe. That vial, the size of a small flashlight, held a liquid so strong it could rip through my system and exit with still enough potency to eat through porcelain. The new reality set in: two killers now waged war inside my body.

And the physical strain was not the toughest part.

Imagine trying to stay focused and determined for seven hours. Not cheerful, just positive as you sit in a chair, needles prodding you from the outside, poison tearing through you on the inside—and cancer battling back. Outside the door is a hallway filled with bodies and minds fighting the same fight.

You are all in the heat of a death battle. One killer against another—chemo versus cancer. There will be only one survivor and you have to take a side, though neither side is a friend.

There are no weekends, no days off, no breaks with cancer. And the chemo—the thing designed to cure you—is actually the toughest part of the fight. Yet, even during the most gruesome, painful moments, I remembered the gritty truth of Kori's whisper. It was a truth I had known all my life.

If I was being forced to fight this deadly opponent, I would fight it my way. Not lying around the house or in bed with my fingers crossed, hoping I would get through it. I was not going to let some faceless monster steal my life without a fierce battle. I would not let the cancer dictate how or how long I lived.

I would grit my teeth and endure the torture every three weeks.

When I wasn't getting treatment, I would do the things I loved. Each morning I woke Kori and Beau and made them breakfast. I studied game films and scouting reports to prepare for ESPN's NFL Draft Day coverage. I worked out five times a week, played the entire season of my basketball league, and prepared to compete in a Fourth of July 5K run for charity.

I ate extremely healthy foods and stuck flawlessly to my workout routine because I wanted to give myself the best chance to survive. The doctors and nurses urged me to drink as much water as I could after each treatment to help flush out the toxins. I knew working out would further push the chemicals from my body.

All my life I believed it was up to me to take action to reach my goals. I'd believed it since I was a boy. Along the way I discovered that within this basic human initiative lies the most common trait of extraordinary people: the will to find a way to victory no matter the obstacle.

It was the same philosophy that allowed me to go from a small-town college in Pocatello, Idaho, to starting for the great

Chuck Noll and the legendary Pittsburgh Steelers. Before that, it allowed me to overcome more common but often unspoken obstacles like my father's abuse, a crippling boyhood accident, and the early loss of my mother.

I was a twelve-year old boy when I stood on my bed and tacked a note card to the corkboard wall behind the headboard that read: "I will play in the NFL." It was like a moment of truth. As I stared at it I could hear all the responses I'd already received from parents, coaches, friends, and brothers. All had a similar reply.

"Don't put all your eggs in one basket, Merril."

"A lot of kids have that dream, Merril. But you have to be realistic, too."

"Do you know how hard that is, Merril?"

Their words bounced around my head like a thousand tiny rubber balls. I realized right then that I could accept everyone else's message to me or I could listen to my own. I hopped off my bed and picked up another note card. In capital letters, I made another note of the three words that popped into my head. I jumped back onto my bed and tacked it at the highest point on the wall I could reach. It read: "FIND A WAY."

In the end, that boyhood vow saw me through more than my obstacles to the NFL. It was no coincidence that as I grew taller and could reach higher, the one note card remained posted atop all my other notes, the peak of what would become a pyramid of handwritten goals.

Those three words taught me that regardless of past or present circumstances, your future path is not paved before you. You pave it as you go, and the materials you use are up to you.

You can pave it with fear, apathy, and self-pity.

Or you can pave it with courage, resilience, and an undying spirit.

The gift bestowed to every one of us is our will. It can be given away but it cannot be taken away, no matter what. And at the end of every day—and every life—what you have done with this gift determines whether you are an ordinary or extraordinary person. The extraordinary find a way.

Each time I sat in that treatment facility, Red Death pulsing through my body, I knew I could not turn away from the philosophy that had given me my dreams. At age thirty-eight, with my life on the line, it was again up to me to find a way to victory.

I did.

Now I want to show you how.

The critical lessons are straightforward. You will understand them cognitively right away. Application comes next. This is the real battle. I do not believe we learn anything new until we can apply it successfully, continuously, in our own lives.

My goal, then, is not to merely tell you how to find a way. I will show you how by giving you a front row seat to some of the greatest battles in my own life. The battles encompass the years before, during, and after my eight years in the NFL.

While playing professional ball was the hard-won culmination of a lifelong dream, many of the obstacles outside the NFL posed a greater challenge. In fact, had I not overcome some of my early battles, my NFL dream would not have become a reality. Had I not won certain victories in the NFL, I would not have overcome the challenges after it.

Embodying the "find a way" philosophy became second nature to me because I would not accept defeat, not because someone taught me the ten steps to success. This book is therefore about transcendent lessons learned the hard way—the real way—through gritty, gutsy action in spite of opponents or odds.

Through these lessons you will come to see that you are not defined by how many times you fall but by how many times you rise again. You might fall a thousand times, but if you rise a thousand times plus one you will be victorious. I carry this mindset with me wherever I go, in whatever I do. Victory is never the absence of failure. It is the will to be the last one standing.

This is no easy task. But every one of us is able.

I was never a great student. I did, however, excel in one subject: statistics. The proficiency has helped me in my new day job as an NFL analyst on ESPN. But I've learned that no matter how many numbers you crunch—no matter how small the odds of victory might be—no amount of statistical evidence can account for the variable of the human spirit.

When the numbers say it can't be done, when history says it has never been done—one undying spirit can rewrite the books and change history forever. One undying spirit can always find a way to victory.

I won't pretend to know what challenges you have faced in your life, or what challenges you are facing now. If we were sitting down together, I would ask you about them and listen. But the truth is that I don't need to know the specifics to assure you that you can find a way to victory. "What lies behind us and what lies before us," wrote Ralph Waldo Emerson, "are tiny matters compared to what lies within us." How true these words have been in my life.

They are also true in yours.

The journey we will take from here will be entertaining, for sure. It will give you a rare look at the world of the NFL and what it took to survive and thrive in one of its storied franchises, the Pittsburgh Steelers. But I encourage you to push yourself beyond the intrigue and entertainment inside these pages. The stories I share were not chosen for their dramatic value. They were chosen for their ability to illustrate the emotions, choices, and actions required to break through to victory despite the obstacles.

Our experiences vary in detail—we are born into different families, given different skills and opportunities, and forced to face different challenges. Yet we are wired with similar needs and desires. No matter your age or life experience, I know you have dreams. I also know you have fears and anxieties that battle against your hopes and expectations. And, ultimately, I know you want to succeed.

We all have intense reasons to live that are greater than

avoiding death. And we all have intensely significant reasons to reach our dreams that are well beyond enjoying mere fame or fortune. *Finding a way* is about tapping into those core spiritual motives inside of you and taking fierce, resourceful, and consistent action until victory is yours. My hope is that by witnessing how this has played out in my life, you will comprehend how it can play out in yours.

I could spend the next two hundred pages filling your mind with every success principle known to man. But once you put this book down, you will still have to find your own way through life's challenges. I would rather show you how I did it so you will know what is possible in your life.

The ability to find a way is within everyone.

2

What Makes a Winner

The year before I was diagnosed with cancer, I read an article about a woman who battled the killer. While I don't remember her name or the circumstances in which I read the article, I do remember one overarching emotion: surrender. The account was like touring medieval dungeons. I set the article down and said to myself, *I'm glad I'll never have to fight that battle. I couldn't do it.*

With that, I programmed myself to be defeated by the disease.

I was as healthy as anyone. No one in my family had experienced cancer. In fact, I had never personally known a single person who had suffered from the disease. I had no reason to think I'd get it. Yet I created a major obstacle by surrendering my will to something before the battle began.

I knew better.

In making the vow, I was focusing my energy on circumstances I wanted to avoid, thus sapping energy from circumstances I wanted to embody. This was the reason I took the news so hard that day in the doctor's office—even harder when my oncologist called our cabin in Idaho to confirm it was non-Hodgkin's lymphoma.

It took Kori's reminder to flip the switch in me. When she echoed the words *find a way* back to me, I flipped from focusing my energy on what I did not want to happen—pain, suffering, death—to focusing my energy on what I *had* to have happen—beating the cancer and living my life.

This is a critical point most people overlook. Your personal resources—attitudes, strengths, skills—always follow in the wake of your mental, emotional, and spiritual focus. If you fixate on avoiding pain, failure, or death, you won't have the resources to pursue pleasure, victory, and life.

You must flip a switch and focus your energy on the things you want to see happen—the childhood dreams...the desired relationships...the daily, monthly, and yearly accomplishments.

When you do, the strength of your skills and force of your will become tangible tools. You wield them as necessary. And they produce.

The best opportunities come into focus.

Goals change from pipe dreams to possibilities.

There is nothing magical about this. Your beliefs about what can and cannot happen in your life tend to be self-fulfilling. Where your energy flows, your resources follow. To find a way to victory in any circumstance, you have to focus your energy where it matters.

When cancer first came after me, I didn't flip the switch. My focus was off and I was already beaten. Once I refocused, I found a way to beat the ruthless killer.

While the fierce battle ensued, I sat alone in recliners for hours at a time and reflected on the rocky path that taught me how to win. . . .

Adulthood began for me when I was a boy growing up in Idaho. I still recall the conversation in which my father laid out the one ground rule in our home: he and my mom would provide lunch money but nothing more. If I wanted anything else—clothes, toys, funds for extracurricular activities—it would come out of my pocket. My older brother, Rick, heard the same rule a few years earlier; my two younger brothers would hear it a little later.

While my mother was her own strong woman who subtly guided us in her own way, when under my father's shadow we could do little but comply.

There were times when it felt as though my father resented his family—although I don't believe this was ever the case. As I matured, I came to see he was just a hardworking man who had his own ideas of what it meant to be a good father—going to work every day and providing food and shelter for his family. What I wanted, however, was his affection and involvement in my life, just being around to teach me about sports and walk me through the curiosities, questions, and challenges of youth. As it was, he left the house before dawn and rarely returned before bedtime. He loved us in his own way, but that way left me wanting for something I couldn't explain back then.

I remember the one vacation we ever took, to California. The highlight of the trip was seeing the ocean. We had only seen pictures. We drove fifteen hours in our green Buick Skylark, the four of us boys compressed into the backseat like oversized luggage. When we finally arrived, unable to contain our excitement, we jumped out of the car. My dad then snapped us to attention.

"Now listen up," he asserted. "Don't go get wet or get sand all over yourselves. I don't want it all over this car."

My father had worked hard for that car. On the one hand I understood that he didn't want the car filled with the remnants of four sweaty, sandy boys. On the other hand, we were young boys who had never seen the ocean.

Growing up it seemed the things that should have mattered got lost in the grind. And those that didn't really matter, mattered more than they should.

I look back now and see how it was then, years before I pressed the philosophy onto my corkboard wall, that I began learning to find a way.

I started throwing newspapers when I was eight years old. I would come home after school, roll the papers, then put them in a pocketed vest that hung over my chest and back. The problem was that with all eighty papers in the vest, I could not lift it. My mother had to hold it up and place it over my head.

The other problem was that I could not stay balanced on a

bike while wearing the vest. If I teetered slightly, the bike and I went down. For two years I walked my paper route because I could not ride it. I had to be strategic about it. I could empty only about ten papers from the front vest pocket before the weight shifted to the back pocket and pulled the neckline of the vest against my throat. It was still too heavy to lift, so in order to breathe, and continue on my route, I had to sit down, crawl out of the vest, and then crawl back in with the back pocket in the front. I had to do this multiple times until I got the number of papers in the vest to an amount I could manage, which was about half the original load.

Resourcefulness forced its hand on me before I knew what it was. This taught me many lessons, but the greatest was a clear understanding of cause and effect. As a kid, I knew things didn't just happen. People made them happen.

I shared a room with my younger brother, Marty, for as long as I could remember. But when I was twelve, I learned I was getting my own room when my dad finished one of the basement bed-rooms. This initiated an early coming-of-age. My own space, my own nights filled with my own thoughts—these compelled me to move dreams from my head and heart to my hands and feet. I needed a way to initiate the transfer.

My one request was that one wall in my new room be covered with corkboard. When my dad asked me why, I told him I wanted a place to pin my goals up so I could see them every morning when I woke and every night before I went to sleep. The day finally came when the room was ready. All I could think about was getting in there and putting up my goals. In fact, I had already written them out on eight-by-ten cards: life goals, yearly goals, and monthly goals. Goals describing how much I wanted to weigh and what I needed to lift and how fast I needed to run. But the one goal above every other goal was to play in the NFL. Above that was: "FIND A WAY."

I slid my bed against that corkboard wall and let my penciled proclamations and the clippings of athletes I admired surround my head while I slept. They were a constant reminder to take actions that mattered.

That summer, I began working on a large farm moving irrigation pipes. I could make $2.50 a line, which was comprised of thirty-two pipes that were each twenty-eight feet long. My goal was to be standing in the fields by five a.m. and spend four hours moving eight lines. Then spend another four hours in the evening moving the same eight lines to their next location. If I did it seven days a week all summer, I would earn enough money to pay for school clothes and a lot more.

I had no idea what I was getting into. Farmers possess a restrained wisdom; they know the important lessons of life come much quicker when a boy is left alone with only a goal and his own devices.

I donned my boots that first day and stepped onto the potato fields to survey the scene. The quarter-mile lines looked a mile long, but the three-inch pipe did not seem very big and the soil did not look very muddy. Then I took another step. The mud crawled up and over the tops of my knee-high boots. The ground was like quicksand.

It took forever to empty my boots and slog my way to the middle of the first pipe. I reached down and yanked. It felt as if it was bolted to the center of the earth. I didn't understand that a three-inch aluminum pipe, twenty-eight feet long and full of water, could weigh up to three hundred pounds.

I tugged, twisted, and pried the pipe every which way I could think of, to no avail. I then hunched over with my hands on my knees and did what felt right. I cried. I was counting on taking thirty minutes to move each of the eight lines—four hours total. Now I was forty-five minutes into the ordeal and hadn't moved a single pipe.

I melted onto the muddy field beneath the gray before dawn and sulked. There was no way I was going to move sixteen quarter-mile lines every day. How would I buy school clothes? How would I pay for the stuff I needed for sports—cleats, pads, and wristbands?

As my sulking fell to despair, the sun reached over the horizon. Golden light framed the fields and flickered on the lines. I lifted my head and remembered the corkboard wall. The pictures of ball players and bodybuilders, my handwritten cards, and the one note posted above all the others.

I pushed myself up and brushed the mud from my pants.

There was a way to do this and I would find it.

I looked down the line to the last pipe in the distance and then back at the first pipe lying heavy at my feet. Suddenly it came to me.

If I separated each pipe from the main line, I could lighten the load. I went to the end of the first pipe in the line, unlatched it and then jiggled it until it came free. I then lifted it as high as I could, which wasn't high, until the water came pouring out. The weight of the pipe was then manageable enough to pull from the mud and move it. I repeated this for each pipe in each line until all eight lines were moved over eighteen rows of spuds.

Until I was a little bigger, it still took me six hours to move eight lines in the morning, and another six hours to move eight more in the evening. Leaving and returning home in the dark was not uncommon that summer. But I cared less about the light of day than the lesson learned. What seemed impossible was possible. And the only difference was a matter of perspective and focus.

When I thought I could not, I did not. When I thought I must, I did.

Having to make my own money, I remained a busy kid year-round. By the time I turned twelve, summers consisted of work and work alone. I would get up at four-thirty every morning and my day would not end until ten p.m. During the school year, I managed to squeeze in some fun. Having three brothers helped the cause. I also managed to get into trouble—this often coming in tight succession with the fun. But the lessons of failure were better learned outside the home than in it.

My father was a hardworking man, as I said, but he was equally hard-nosed. This was good to an extent, but when he was home it conveyed the wrong message: I don't have time for your fun or your foolishness. He spent most of his downtime alone, watching the television or reading the paper in his recliner. We learned very early not to interfere.

My father always used the excuse that he was treated the same way. He knew no different. I probably would have accepted my father's excuse if I never had kids of my own. But I now have two and I cannot comprehend treating them like he did us.

When I first laid eyes on Kori, my firstborn, an emotion so strong rose up in me that I cannot explain it other than to say I wanted more than anything in the world to protect her and prepare her for a good, long life.

This is the dilemma all excuse makers face: if you are a victim of your circumstances—if you "know no different"—how then does someone in the same circumstances forge a higher path? What makes that difference?

One word: responsibility.

Until a person takes responsibility for the path before him, he will constantly ask "Why me?" of the path behind him. This defers his focus and thus his resources to something he cannot change—the past: *Why did this happen to me? Why didn't this happen to me instead?*

As a result, he won't find the resources to improve the present. He will lose sight of all resourcefulness.

Though I was only a kid, I could see the great inconsistencies in my father's life. I would not be able to expound on them until I was older, but before I was a teen, I knew I did not want to carry on his paternal legacy. I wanted to become a different

25

man—a present, loving father and a responsible, resilient leader. I knew no one had more control over these results than I did.

My father's shortcomings taught me an early lesson about personal responsibility. While I made many of my own mistakes growing up, I never tried to skirt the issue by blaming past or present circumstances. I had seen my father do this all along. I had seen the damage it caused him, and those around him.

I was by no means a brilliant kid, but I learned that to be a winner—to accomplish the things I set out to accomplish—I had to own all my decisions regardless of what had or had not happened in my life. This mind-set would allow me to break the chain in my family. Before I would have that opportunity, it allowed me to forge a path to many other significant victories. Each one prepared me and progressed me toward the greater battles to come.

I'm a firm believer that in life you wrestle with either the pains of regret or the pains of resilience. The great difference is where the wrestling leads you.

My father wrestles with the pains of regret to this day. He called me in 2003 when I was diagnosed with cancer to apologize in his own way. Then he told me he had another family now and needed to focus on them. I was not particularly shocked by his words. He has seen Kori three times and Beau only once. His two grandchildren are now in their teens.

Unlike my father, I vowed to wrestle with only the pains of resilience. With my three-word strategy posted above my bed,

I kept making progress. As I approached high school, I held the will of a man and the lessons of a lifetime inside a fourteen-year-old body. They were needed. More obstacles stood in my way than I could imagine.

The summer before my freshman year I was back in the potato fields, moving lines with my brother Marty. By this time, modernity had caught on and manually moving every line was no longer necessary. Some pipes were wheeled and entire lines could be moved via a motorized tower positioned in the middle of the quarter-mile line. The motorized tower used a series of cogs and chains to create enough torque to lift, turn, and drive entire lines to a new position in the field. My job with these lines was to manage each wheel tower to ensure it did its job.

Before that day, I had seen the tremendous power these machines generated. I had seen pipe wheels get stuck in the mud and the churning tower snap a metal line like a dead branch. Still, managing the tower's job was typically a straightforward task. But on July 2, the task changed.

The largest cogwheel on one of my towers was misaligned. This was normally something we would have fixed before moving the lines, but in order to get July 3 and 4 off, we had to move the lines on the second. I couldn't spend the evening taking apart and reassembling the tower. I had to make do. So to ensure the misaligned tower did its job, my boss and I decided I could simply press the big cogwheel against the smaller cogwheels as it rolled across the field.

As the sun descended, I was walking alongside the broken tower, pressing on the face of the large cogwheel to keep it in place. I then felt something running down the bare skin of my back beneath my shirt. I turned around and looked up. Mud was dripping from above. I thought of my mom's challenge to me to keep my clothes clean that day, so I reached behind me with my right hand and wiped the mud from the tower.

Before my eyes returned to the big cogwheel, I felt a sudden jerk on my left arm. Then a crushing sound like Styrofoam in a meat grinder.

My eyes shot to the cogwheel. My left hand was being fed in and crushed between a smaller cogwheel and chain.

I couldn't believe it was attached to my body.

Within two seconds, the machine had eaten my hand as my wrist, elbow, and shoulder joints contorted in a paltry attempt to ease the massive force. Another quarter turn of the cogwheel and one or more joints was going to give. Then the machine suddenly stopped. I didn't know if it was jammed with my limb or if it had died.

I could not reach the kill switch so I unthinkingly swatted the bar that releases the tension on the chain. A bolt of panic shot through me as I realized what I had done. When that bar is released, the cogs and chains immediately spin backward like wound-up propellers. My entire arm was about to be sucked in the other way and shredded like a limb in a chipper.

As panic blinked into terror, the chain suddenly froze and the tower stalled. In all my months of working with those towers, I had never seen a chain not release. And I had never seen

28

the machine completely stall—not even when a three-inch metal pipe was caught in the mechanism. It was a miracle that my arm was not ripped from the socket.

I stared at my hand. It was mangled and still trapped between the small cogwheel and chain. Blood was squirting everywhere.

Somehow at that moment I did not panic. But one thought shot through my head: *Without a left hand, I will never play football again.*

I calmly called to my brother, who was standing at the end of the line.

By the time he arrived, a large pool of blood stained the dirt at my feet.

Marty started screaming.

Thirty minutes earlier and twenty miles away, my boss stood from the table in the middle of dinner.

"Where are you going?" his wife asked.

"I need to check on Merril," he replied.

Like an angel from God, his blue Chevy pickup came rumbling onto the muddy field minutes after the accident. It was the first time he'd ever checked on me in two years.

He removed the chain from the cogwheel and gently withdrew my pulverized limb. Blood started to gush. We rushed to the hospital.

My digits looked like strips of ground beef. It took ten hours of surgery and 120 stitches to reattach three fingers and sew my hand back together. A portion of my pinkie could not be saved.

In the middle of the night, I woke up alone in a hospital and looked out the window next to my bed. I was still groggy but I could see all the stars in the sky, and my first thought was that I was dead. Then I started to remember what had happened.

My heart started pounding and I looked down at my hand. I saw only a ball of gauze. The end was stained in dark blood. I felt nothing.

I started screaming.

I thought they had amputated my hand.

The classic 1980 film *The Shining* popularized an ancient Egyptian proverb when its villain's descent into insanity was encapsulated by the penned phrase, "All work and no play makes Jack a dull boy." It would take two years for my hand to return to normal use but only two minutes in a hospital bed for me to understand the meaning of that phrase.

Until the accident, work had defined my days—job work, schoolwork, and homework. Before most of my friends held their first jobs, I had a half decade of experience. The lessons were incalculable. Yet each year of labor had dulled my childhood passion.

As I sat in that hospital bed and stared at my hand wrapped in bloody cloth—wrapped in a fist that made it look like a stump—I realized I had the rest of my life to work, and only a small window of opportunity to do what I loved for a living: play football.

From that moment on, I had tunnel vision. I would do whatever it took to become the best football player I could be.

Manual jobs became opportunities to strengthen my football muscles. Mental jobs, including schoolwork, became opportunities to sharpen my football mind. Later I would look back and glean the additional lessons of that season, but for a long stretch I was blinded to all but that which moved me closer to playing in the NFL.

Armed with resourcefulness beyond my years, I knew achieving my goal would still take every bit of effort and enthusiasm I had—and some help from God. But I had been the underdog all my life—the farm boy bound to work hard but unlikely to be the hero. The role didn't bother me. It only stoked my fire.

Approximately 100,000 high school seniors play football every year. Only 0.2 percent make an NFL roster.[1] The road to the NFL is a tight tunnel designed to squeeze out all but the elite players. It helps to have a good name and a great arm but, ultimately, finding the light at the end of the narrow pass takes more than pedigree and skill.

Over the course of my football career, I would learn precisely what that "more" meant.

Before high school I was a talented quarterback, but when I discovered our high school team would feature a running offense, I knew I had to switch positions. I became a running back. I not only started; I excelled. Coaches took notice. I was on my way. So I thought.

Then I started to grow cocky. I already had a strained relationship with the coaches because work prohibited me from attending summer practices. They didn't like it and hadn't bothered to ask why, and so I looked as if I just didn't care. I didn't like that they never cared enough to ask me what was going on. So when my sophomore year began, they had their reservations about me, and I had a chip on my shoulder. I started acting like an idiot.

I could run circles around the other players on the team, so I started showing up late for practice and taking my helmet off and sitting on it after finishing drills well ahead of everyone else. My childish actions quickly came back to haunt me.

On a Thursday, the day before the fifth game of my sophomore year, a friend and I decided to skip school and go deer hunting, then return in time for practice. We got caught in a snowstorm and missed practice altogether.

Because of the snowstorm our team cancelled practice, but the head coach had roll call after school. When he called my name and I didn't answer, my teammates confessed, "He's hunting."

"Then Merril won't be playing in the game tomorrow," our head coach stated.

When I got word of this the next morning at school, I walked straight to the head coach's classroom and asked him if I was going to play that night.

"No," he replied.

"Fine," I said, "then I quit!"

"Good," he said, "I was thinking of kicking you off anyway!"

Once off the football team, I maintained the momentum by quitting the basketball team a couple of months later. I was on a roll.

It was the best thing that could happen to me at that time.

A few weeks into the basketball season, I attended the big game between our high school, Highland, and our crosstown rival, Pocatello (or "Poky") High. I was late and by myself, and as I walked through the double doors of the gym, I spotted all my friends on the court playing. At that precise moment, one of my closest friends sunk a critical shot. As he and my other friends celebrated, it hit me. After committing myself to do whatever it took to become the best athlete I could be, I was suddenly on the outside looking in.

And I had no one to blame but myself.

Even though I could not attend summer practices and the coaches weren't as understanding as they could have been, I was being a baby about the whole thing. I was feeling sorry for myself and carrying on to the point that no matter how good an athlete I was, my teams were better off without me. From that point on, I made sure a pity party never got in my way again. I went back to my coaches and apologized for my bad attitude. The following year I would be back in business playing both sports, with football being my main focus.

In the meantime, I still needed to make money. Until that point, I hadn't seen that there were other job options besides working on the farm. I applied at a grocery store and got a job as a bagger. My hours freed me up so that I could make a lot of the summer practices, but the money was not enough to cover my expenses. I was driving now, and buying my own gas took a lot of my paycheck. Marty and I decided to look for work we could do together.

We found a job cleaning a large office building every night during the week. The good part was that it was a late weeknight job that would allow me to make every practice and play in every game. The hard part was that the building was huge and we had to take out all the trash from everyone's office, scrub every toilet and mop every bathroom floor, vacuum all the carpets, and buff all the other hard floors. The other hard part was that the only time we could do the job was immediately after practice.

By the time my junior year rolled around, Marty and I were like machines on the job. It would take us four hours to complete everything. Once practice was over, we would throw on our cleaning clothes and head straight to the building. Our only pit stop was the Arctic Circle drive-thru. We often had enough money for only one hamburger, but a good friend who worked there would sneak us a free bag of fries. That food would carry us until we got home between ten and ten-thirty.

Even though I spent more hours working than playing, football remained on my mind throughout the day. I was eager to put my sophomore year behind me. Once the summer passed and my junior season arrived, I vowed to redeem myself on the field.

I then tore my groin on a kickoff during the first game. I returned eight weeks later and injured my quad. When the season ended, I had played only one game. Suddenly my future was in a precarious situation. It wasn't the way I had planned it.

Due to a combination of selfishness and unforeseen injury, I was going into my senior season having never played a full season of high school ball. Furthermore, I missed all but one game of the most important season where scholarships were concerned—my junior year.

I did not know if a single college would give me a look. But I couldn't control that. I vowed to focus my resources on the only thing I could control: each and every game of my senior season.

I played like a man possessed. Despite painful bumps and bruises, I stayed on the field all season and produced. I was selected as the team's MVP and the top running back in the state. With everything on the line and no margin for error, that was the year I learned the critical difference between pain and injury.

Injury sidelines you. Sitting out is necessary because full healing will not occur otherwise. You risk more severe damage if you play with injury.

Pain is a different animal. It is far more common than injury. If you have the will, you can always find a way to play with pain. And what is most interesting is that the more you learn to play with pain, the fewer injuries you seem to sustain.

This fact would define my football career from then on. Pain would never again keep me from my goals.

After my senior season, there were no longer questions about my heart. I wore it on my jersey sleeves. I wanted to play. And I would play hard. The combination was enough to garner one offer—from Idaho State, an unknown Division I-AA college in my hometown.

I took what I was given and ran with it. One opportunity was all I sought.

I'm a great believer in luck," Thomas Jefferson once quipped, "and I find that the harder I work the more I have of it." At Idaho State, I was unknown and unrecognized. I was one of two running backs offered a scholarship and one of eight running backs on the team. There, I could not let up for a second. To be worthy of the NFL, I had to excel beyond anyone before me or around me. Only eleven players had ever been drafted from Idaho State. Only four made it past their second year in the NFL.

I would have to find a way to be more than was expected of a player in that program. I would work harder than I had ever worked. I would play with pain and remain on the field. I would not back down from any challenge. I would do more and be more than the expectations.

This was my subsequent so-called luck: by the end of my senior season, I had set forty-four school and conference records and two NCAA records. I also hadn't missed a game in three years.

NFL scouts were curious. The records and resilience meant something, but they came against no-name players on no-name programs. The begging question was whether I could produce the same results against the best talent on the planet.

Five teams were willing to find out. I worked out for the

Oakland Raiders, Washington Redskins, Green Bay Packers, Denver Broncos, and Pittsburgh Steelers before the draft. I was most impressive in my workout for the Packers. I ran a 4.58 forty, and the scout assured me my stock would go way up. What he didn't know is that I would not break a 4.7 for the other teams. The 4.58 would be seen as an anomaly.

In fact, the Broncos scout could not hide his disappointment. I ran cones and caught passes, then he clocked me in the forty-yard dash on grass, turf, and a track. I ran six times in all and never broke a 4.7. After the last forty, the scout looked at his stopwatch, mumbled something to himself, then shook his head. "You look so much faster on film," he grumbled.

He began stuffing cones into his large duffel bag, complaining about the waste of time. He then looked back up at me and, apparently needing to purge every bit of displeasure, said, "You'll never make it in this league. You're too small and too slow."

The words stung. They felt personal and were a sharp contrast to the response from the Packers scout. In fact, they were a sharp contrast to all the other scouts. The others had at least treated me with common decency. The Steelers scout had even inquired about my off-season interests.

"Do you play basketball?" he asked.

"Yes, sir," I replied.

"The Steelers have a great off-season team," he said. "You can make a little extra money that way."

It was an odd conversation but a cordial one, too. I remembered it specifically because we had discussed basketball far more than football. I genuinely liked the scout but also figured our main topic of discussion meant Pittsburgh was out of the picture. Surely we'd have talked football if they were serious about me.

In the end, though I didn't enjoy it, I was also grateful for the Denver scout's frankness. After the initial disappointment, the words *too small* and *too slow* popped around my head like sparks. They fanned my fire. Instead of packing up my dreams and heading back to Idaho farmland with my tail between my legs, I used the skepticism as fuel.

If the Denver scout was saying the only thing standing between me and the NFL was getting bigger and faster, that was nothing. I knew the way to work harder.

I'd held a man's job since I was a kid. I'd labored on a farm from dark to dark, seven days a week, all summer long. I'd mopped floors and scrubbed toilets after high school football and basketball practice every night for two years. I'd worked six-day, ten-hour shifts for Exxon when I was nineteen. The word *handout* was not in my vocabulary.

After my five predraft workouts, I reviewed the scouting reports on me. They all read: "Self-made player." None said: "Quick, agile, big, and strong." I didn't like that. I wanted those physical traits to be true of me.

I would learn I possessed something more valuable.

My son, Beau, once asked me about what he had to do to be a winner. I explained the importance of physical and mental training. "That," I said, "is the baseline to play the game. But in the end," I continued, "resourcefulness is your greatest resource.

"No matter what skill set you have been blessed with, you must sharpen those skills like a razor blade and then exhaust yourself to become the very best player you can be." I told Beau this did not guarantee he would make it to the NFL or the Hall of Fame. It guaranteed something more important: he would live with no regrets.

"You will be able to lay your head on your pillow every night and know you left nothing to chance. There is tremendous peace in knowing this."

I then described Walter Payton.

"He was not the biggest or the strongest or the fastest running back in the NFL," I asserted. "He was just the best."

3

Attitude Is Not Enough

On the evening of the Fourth of July before my senior year at Idaho State, my mom went to take a shower. She and my dad had just returned from moving my oldest brother and his wife to Seattle. She was weary from the drive and sad her oldest baby was gone. My dad slipped into his recliner in their bedroom and fell fast asleep.

I was watching a fireworks show we had been planning on for weeks when I leaned over to my girlfriend and told her I had to go home. My mother had laid into me that afternoon for not cleaning up the house before she and my dad returned. She had hung up on me and I still felt bad about it.

To my great surprise, my girlfriend understood. I dropped her at home and headed toward mine. As I turned right at the stop sign at the end of my street, I looked to see if our porch lights were on, signifying my parents were still up. Instead I saw red and blue flashing lights.

My first thought was that my dad had suffered a heart attack. When I was younger, his job as a milkman kept him active throughout the week, but when he began to sell insurance a few years earlier, he'd become sedentary and started to gain weight. We had all been saying he was going to have a heart attack if he kept up that lifestyle.

I sped down my street and screeched to the curb between two police cruisers. As I jumped from my car, the front door of our house swung open. The paramedics were wheeling someone out on a gurney. I looked closely and was shocked at what I saw.

It was my mother's lifeless face.

Two paramedics were beside her, working on her chest as they rushed her to the ambulance. A police officer exited the house behind the gurney. My dad was next to him. He looked as if he'd been shot in the gut. The blood rushed from my head and I was weak.

I soon learned that my mother never made it out of the shower. My dad woke from his nap and heard the water still running. He went in to check on her and found her facedown in the tub.

The drain had not been plugged, so she hadn't drowned, but her heart had gone into fibrillation. She'd been lying unconscious and without oxygen for several minutes. The paramedics were able to get her heart started, but it was too late. Her brain was gone. She lay in a coma on life support for twelve days and then passed on July 16.

I still remember the feeling. It was like treading water in

the middle of the ocean. There was nothing substantial to grasp and no land in sight—only a vast, undulating space where my emotions bobbed aimlessly and unsettled. My mom was gone. I was lost.

Though I was not close to my dad, his pain greatly affected me. I would often come upstairs from my room and see him bent over the kitchen sink crying. I didn't know what to do or say. We all took her death hard, but he seemed to take it harder than anyone. I think he blamed himself to an extent. He loved my mom in his own broken-down way, and she offered perhaps the only unconditional love he'd ever known. She was also the glue to our fractured family. With her gone, we had to pick up our own pieces. Some never fit together quite the same.

I was twenty-one when it happened. The circumstances of my life were rapidly shifting into adulthood. While the loss wounded deeply and lingered long, football and my postcollege decisions helped me hang on to a sense of normalcy. Still, there was not a day I didn't miss my mom during my senior year—especially once football season was over and the new year had dawned. I was still living at home, where her void took my breath every minute. As the annual NFL draft approached, a mixture of pride and sadness swirled inside me.

The pride was a reflection of what I knew she'd feel. She would have been so pleased that the NFL scouts and experts were talking about me—some even suggesting I had a chance to go in the second or third round. The sadness was in knowing she would not be around to see this dream unfold. She had read the note cards. She had heard me talk football since I was a small boy. She had watched me work long hours well before my time. She deserved to see the culmination of it all.

Though she was not there, I felt her alongside me, especially as I woke on April 28, 1987, known to many as D-Day: Draft Day.

For 335 college players, the D would also stand for dream fulfilled. For the rest, it would stand for disappointment.

Before the NFL combine, experts were confident I'd go in the first five rounds. After the combine, there were more questions than answers.

The NFL combine is an athletic spectacle. For the athletes participating, it can also be a source of humiliation. One of the first things you do upon arrival is stand alone in your underwear on a makeshift stage as your height, weight, and arm span are measured. You are, of course, only alone in the sense that no one else is in their underwear. The room is in fact filled with personnel from every NFL team, and they are not only observing the procession of athletes but also videotaping it. If you're the least bit modest or don't enjoy being the center of attention, the exercise can be your worst nightmare. The experience reminded me of a cattle auction; the only difference was that I was the cow.

After the measurements are all taken, the athletes are run through a series of tests to determine if all that muscled physique translates into a desirable combination of strength, agility, speed, and smarts. You lie on a bench beneath a 225-pound bar and press the weight as many times as you can. Your best vertical and broad jumps are measured. Machines test the balanced strength of your hamstrings and quadriceps as well as your flexibility. You are also given a Wonderlic test, which measures your applied intellect, then you're asked to attend interviews with interested teams. From there, the on-field drills begin.

You run agility drills like the cone drill and the shuttle drill. Skill drills like passing, route running, and catching. And speed drills like the famous timed forty-yard dash.

All of these tests and drills are spread over several days, and every year someone shows up and shocks scouts with his amazing athletic ability. The media loves to hype up a receiver who records an incredible forty time or a tackle who shows incredible quickness, but the best scouts know the combine alone cannot give you a firm conclusion about a player's ability to play football.

The only thing the combine can do is give teams a measurement of the athletic ability a guy has and some hints about his character. When it comes to whether or not a guy will make a great pro, the safest judgments come from watching him play. I would later learn that this was what intrigued the Steelers about me. It was a good thing, too, because two days before I was to board the plane for Indy, I came down with the flu and lost ten pounds.

I decided to go anyway, and it may not have been the best decision.

For me, the combine was impressive and overwhelming at the same time. I had never been on such a big stage, and I knew no other player there had watched me play on Saturday. I, on the other hand, had watched many of them. In fact, there was subtle yet tangible evidence that they were simply more mature and experienced than I was.

For starters, I had never flown on a plane by myself before that trip. Consequentially, after landing in Indianapolis, I immediately tossed the sleeve of tickets the NFL had given me in the trash. This included my return ticket. Fortunately, the Wonderlic test would not have any air travel questions.

I barely had the strength to stand, let alone endure days of running drills and taking tests. Unfortunately, it showed. I registered a pokey 4.9 forty. A few enormous linemen ran faster. Then when it came time for the one skill I was expected to excel in— pass catching—I embarrassed myself more. The drill required each player to turn his back to a quarterback firing a fifteen-yard pass and wait for a coach to yell, "Ball!" Once you heard the call, the object was to turn around and immediately catch the ball.

The drill not only tested your hands, it tested your hand/eye coordination, because the ball was not merely coming fast, it was on top of you when you turned. The running backs before me had not fared well. Balls ricocheted off their hands, shoulders, and chests. A few went flying by their heads before they could even react.

When my turn came, I was anxious to set myself apart. I took my place, turned my back, and waited for the call.

I heard "Ball!" and twisted around with my hands spread in front of my chest. My reactions were slow.

The ball ricocheted off my forehead. For five seconds I saw double.

I shook it off. It was only one ball. I could make up for it.

I turned around and waited for the next pass.

"Ball!"

I twisted around again, eyes wide and hands ready. Not ready enough.

The ball bounced off my face a second time.

While I fared well in other drills and would go on to have better private workouts, my slow forty time and the two leather bullets to the forehead clouded my professional value.

When I took my seat on the couch to watch the first day of the 1987 draft, I hoped the combine had not hurt my chances more than help them.

Back then the NFL draft did not receive the national coverage that it does now. There were no bloggers or tweeters leaking the inside scoop. If you were a projected mid- to late-rounder, the best you could do was flip on the TV and wait for the phone to ring. This was too nerve-racking for some, and so it wasn't uncommon for players to spend draft days outside busying themselves with menial tasks.

I stayed inside.

Day one passed slowly, anxiously. Rounds 1 and 2 came and went.

It would have been incredible to get the call then, but I didn't expect it. My focus was on Rounds 3 and 4. They arrived and I was on edge. Shifting in my seat. Staring at the phone. Standing up, walking around. Getting food, sitting back down. Ready at the NFL commissioner's announcement of each pick.

Round 3 began. Twenty-nine picks. No calls.

Round 4 passed. Nothing.

The day ended. No calls.

Fifth round, I told myself. *Tomorrow morning I'll get the call.*

I ate dinner and walked to my bedroom. I was confident but slightly less so than before.

I woke early the next morning. This was the day and I knew it.

How early in the fifth round would I go?

I threw some eggs and toast down my throat, flipped on the television, and took my spot alone in the living room.

The fifth round dragged. Then concluded. No calls.

The sixth round passed, and the seventh. Silence.

The eighth round passed.

Then the ninth.

I began to worry. Three more rounds, eighty-four more picks, and the draft was done. Hundreds of talented college players remained undrafted. I was only one of many.

Would I be one of the few?

I stood and walked to my parents' room. There I knelt at my mother's side of the bed and bowed my head.

"Heavenly Father," I prayed, "I've done everything possible to find a way to the NFL. If this is the way I am supposed to go, bless me with a team that needs me and that I can make. If it's not, please help me find another path."

I rose, walked outside, and started playing basketball.

An untainted, uncontrived peace washed over me. Regard-less of the day's outcome, I knew I had worked as hard as I could. I had done my part and did not have any anxiety about some-thing I should have or could have done better. If I was fortunate enough to get to the next level, I was ready. If not, the next step was in God's hands.

I was shooting free throws when the phone rang. My heart accelerated. I sprinted inside.

On the other end was the same scout who had asked me if I played basketball.

"You want to be a Pittsburgh Steeler?" he said.

"Yes sir!"

"You can make this team, Merril. This team needs you."

Had he heard my prayer?

I had given my all for one shot at the NFL. Now the shot was mine.

A minute later, the Steelers drafted me in the tenth round with the 261st pick of the draft. I'll admit that I was a little dis-appointed to have been drafted so late. While I was excited and ready to play ball at the next level, I didn't have a big celebration when I knew it was happening. I went and told my dad, who was in another room. I also called my girlfriend and told her. I then went downstairs, picked up a globe, and located Pittsburgh. When I saw it was close to New York, my eyes widened. *I have to go all that way?*

An hour after the call from the scout, I received another

call from an administrator in the Steelers' front office. I would be boarding a plane for Pittsburgh the next day and I would be spending the night.

My next battle had begun swiftly and immediately. My heart was heavy, but the news lifted it.

I had been fighting for this opportunity a long time. Despite my anxiety about the unknowns, I committed myself to the challenge of leaving Idaho for a big city two thousand miles away. Over the next few weeks, I would sell my car, my snow skis, my hunting equipment, and anything else I could not pack in a suitcase.

I was not coming back.

I could have counted on two hands the number of travelers in the small Pocatello airport the following day when I boarded a plane for the big city of Pittsburgh. The flight—only the third of my life—went by quickly as a million thoughts sped the time along. As we went into our descent, I peered out the window in amazement at all the hills and trees. It was this green: I actually wondered if it was the location where all the Tarzan movies were filmed. My entire life had been spent in the West. I knew wide deserts and massive mountain ranges and big skies that stretched for miles. This place I was flying into was another world in more ways than I imagined.

My ears were clogged and my nerves were jumping as I deplaned into what looked to me like an anthill of humanity. I looked around to see if someone noticed me.

A stocky man with jet-black hair and dark eyebrows looked my way and approached. He stretched out his hand.

"Merril," he said, "I'm Dick Hoak, the Steelers' running backs coach. Welcome to Pittsburgh."

Coach Hoak was a Pittsburgh icon. Born thirty miles east of the Steel City in Jeannette, Pennsylvania, he was a standout running back at a local high school and then at Penn State in the late fifties and early sixties. He was drafted in the seventh round by the Steelers in 1961. He excelled as a Pro Bowl player until his retirement in 1970. Hoak was the Steelers' number two all-time rusher when he hung up his cleats.

Chuck Noll hired Dick Hoak as the Steelers' running backs coach in 1972 (he would remain in this position for thirty-four years, the longest tenure of any coach in Steelers history). When he picked me up that day, Coach Hoak had already been with the Steelers organization as a player and coach longer than I had been alive.

As we drove away from the airport, he skipped the small talk. He launched into a discussion about numbering systems for offensive plays. I couldn't quite hear everything he was saying because the pressure in my ears hadn't released. But not wanting to look stupid or disrespectful, I still gave an answer each time I knew Coach Hoak asked a question. It wasn't until minicamp that I learned what I affirmed and what I should have corrected.

Coach Hoak dropped me at my hotel and gave me instructions about my dinner pickup. An hour later I was driven to an upscale restaurant on Mount Washington, where I joined the other Steelers draftees. The premier hilltop community is perched above the southern side of the Pittsburgh skyline. The view is the best in the state. From any spot you can watch the southwestern Allegheny and Monongahela rivers rolling into the Ohio River to give the region its famous "Three Rivers" identity. The many city lights glowing and reflecting off windowed buildings and rivers looked like Christmastime. It was appropriate. This was a celebration, after all—our welcome to the great city of Pittsburgh, welcome to the great Steelers franchise. I couldn't believe I was there.

My fellow draftees, including future NFL stars Rod Woodson, Thomas Everett, Hardy Nickerson, and Greg Lloyd, wore designer suits, expensive ties, and crocodile skin shoes. I had seen most of them play on television. They had not seen me. They would remember me still. I donned hush puppies, tan slacks, and a navy-blue, one-button blazer with a white hankie blooming from the pocket—a tad short of overalls and a pitchfork. I was far from home.

On Mount Washington the rookies were introduced to the NFL in much classier style than we would be a couple months later. Filling the restaurant were the finest materials, finest food, and finest service. Most of the coaches and front office executives were there to meet and greet us, but to this day I cannot recall the details of the night. I was spinning in the unfamiliar sights and sounds, like Crocodile Dundee in Manhattan.

Afterward, the sirens and traffic sounds outside my room kept me awake most of the night. I'd never heard so much noise. But sleep mattered little. I'd been looking forward to the next morning more than anything. We would receive a tour of Three

Rivers. It would be my first visit to any professional team's stadium.

Back then teams didn't have their front offices, training facilities, and stadiums in separate locations. Most housed them under one roof. Three Rivers was no different. The Steelers practiced on the same field in which they played their home games, dressed in one locker room beneath the stadium, and conducted business in offices within the stadium's outer shell.

I joined the other draftees at the west entrance the following morning. While we waited, I looked up at the massive structure and then beyond it, at the Ohio River in the distance with the West End Bridge reaching across it. I scanned the parking lot and imagined cars filling the spaces and buzzing fans filing into the stadium. My heart thumped against my ribs as I realized they would soon be watching me on the field just inside those walls.

We entered through glass double doors into a well-appointed lobby. We were immediately confronted by a large glass case. Glistening and prominent inside it were the team's four sterling-silver Lombardi trophies from Super Bowls IX, X, XIII, and XIV. They represented the most Super Bowl wins of any NFL team at that time. Just beyond them was a reception desk sitting beneath a huge mural of the Steel Curtain defense. All the famous faces were there: "Mean" Joe Greene, L. C. Greenwood, Ernie Holmes, Dwight White, Jack Ham, Jack Lambert, Mel Blount, and the rest of the legendary defense of the seventies.

We stood for a moment and stared. I studied the design: a regulation-size football atop what resembles an elongated kicking tee, the napkin brainstorm of Oscar Riedner, then vice president of design for Tiffany & Co., while sitting beside NFL commissioner Pete Rozelle at a luncheon.[1] I read the inscriptions on each trophy: the date of the victory and the game's final score. Twice the Steelers had won back-to-back Super Bowls in the 1970s, first in '74 and '75 and again in '78 and '79.

Right then it hit me: this was no ordinary franchise and no ordinary opportunity. Three hundred and thirty-five players had been drafted that year but only twelve by the Pittsburgh Steelers. I wondered if my fellow draftees felt it the way I did.

Our guide pointed to our right and led us down a hall containing all the coaches' offices and meeting rooms. At the end of the hall we hung a left and then a quick right, where our path opened to a much wider and longer hall. Near the end was a set of steel double doors. Our guide pulled them open and we entered the locker room.

Black and gold were everywhere. I immediately scanned the room for names I knew—the names any football fan knew. My eyes stuck on John Stallworth's nameplate. I recalled his game-changing touchdown against the Los Angeles Rams in Super Bowl XIV. With the Steelers trailing the Rams 19–17 in the fourth quarter, Bradshaw unleashed a bomb to the lanky receiver. Stallworth caught it and outran his defender for a seventy-three-yard touchdown that would pave the way for the Steelers' fourth championship. I noticed his helmet hanging in his locker. The eight-year-old in me wanted to put it on.

Rodgers Freyvogel, the assistant equipment manager at the time, pointed me to a locker with my nameplate above it. I stared at it for a few seconds, then glanced at the locker next to mine.

54

The nameplate read Donnie Shell. He was probably the hardest-hitting safety of all time. I remembered watching the famous hit he once put on Earl Campbell. The big back had run at will for most of the game, but on one particular play he ran smack into the Steelers line and tried to spin into daylight. Before he could square his shoulders upfield, Shell hurled himself into Campbell's thick frame, fracturing the back's ribs and knocking him out of the game.

Rodgers leaned over to me and interrupted my thoughts.

"By the way," he said, nodding to my locker, "this used to be Franco's locker."

My knees nearly buckled.

The players spent several minutes surveying the locker room and adjacent training facility, known as one of the premier facilities in the United States. I felt a mix of anticipation and anxiety. *What will it be like in here? Pro Bowl players sitting next to twenty-two-year-old rookies—will we get along? Am I supposed to just shut up and do my job? Will we be friends or will it be every man for himself?*

Our guides then instructed us to don the new shorts and helmets hanging in our lockers. We walked out the steel doors into the hall and up the players' ramp to the field.

As I stood there, inside Three Rivers, I was struck by the contrast between the college stadiums where I'd stood before and this new place I'd play in. Three Rivers was different. I felt like an ant in the Grand Canyon.

My heart pumped. Some of the greatest players of all time

bent the turf where I stood. Some of the NFL's most memorable plays spilled out in the space between the seats. The stadium was empty, and we could hear the ground crew bustling around, lining the diamond and preparing the field for the next Pirates home game. Before long, the crew would begin preparing the field for football. More memories would be made.

Training camp was only two months away.

T ime," wrote the Swiss novelist Max Frisch, "does not change us. It just unfolds us." The next eight weeks unfolded the larger battle that would define me for the next eight years: the battle to move from surviving to thriving... from putting on a uniform to playing the game at the highest level.

My time in the NFL would pass simultaneously like a day and a lifetime. I held to my dream tightly but had to pick it up anew each morning because there were always circumstances that threatened to end it.

It is this way with all dreams. There is the price you pay to get them, and there is the price you pay to keep them. The prices are never the same. Often dreams are much harder to sustain than they were to gain.

In my case, there were lessons to be learned—lessons that had to be learned for me to remain in the league longer than the vast majority who were out in three and a half years or less. This was stage one of my battle: be good enough, smart enough, and tough enough to keep my dream of being a professional football player.

Stage two of my battle was about succeeding. My dream was never to merely make it to the NFL. I wanted to make an impact. I wanted to be remembered. Only time would tell how far I could go. My resolve would be tested from day one.

There was a little saying going around the locker room on the first day of training camp: "You can't make the club in the tub." I remembered thinking it would never apply to me. A dislocated shoulder kept me out of a couple of games during my freshman year at Idaho State, but since then pain had not kept me from a game. I planned on keeping the three-year streak alive.

There were some things I didn't plan for.

Finally slipping into my Steelers helmet and full pads for some real action felt like Christmas and winning the lottery at the same time. The exhilaration remained until I entered my first live huddle of training camp.

Across from me was Hall of Fame center Mike Webster. I glanced up at his helmet. It looked as if it had been attacked by a grizzly bear. Chunks of fiberglass were missing all over the dome and the rubber was peeling off the facemask. I spied the other helmets in the huddle. The only squeaky clean ones were atop the rookies' green heads. All the veterans' helmets were dulled with deep gouges and colored scuffs from the paint of opponent's helmets, like cars after many collisions. They were symbols of a new level of intensity I was about to experience.

Five minutes and a few huddles later, Coach Noll called a play to me, a P-10, a quick trap between the right guard and center. It was my first chance to prove myself worthy of a draft pick.

I accelerated at the snap and squeezed the ball tightly in my arms. The hole opened up beautifully in front of me. My eyes widened as I exhaled and turned on the afterburners and then—*CRACK!* I was blindsided by a huge defensive tackle named Darryl Sims.

Two things happened in that moment. One, the incredible quickness and power of the game became crystal clear. Second, Sims hit me so hard he separated the scar tissue still in my ribs from fracturing them the year before. I couldn't breathe as I lay beneath his body.

I knew I could not afford to be hurt in the first practice of my professional life, so I pushed myself up and rejoined the huddle. I then held my breath for the next two hours. Every movement felt like daggers in my abdomen.

When I returned to the locker room after practice, I pressed on my ribs and subtly assessed the pain. It was unbearable and I was nauseous, but I told no one. I went to the team dinner and the final meeting as if everything was normal.

Before I lay down that night, I contemplated slipping into the training room tub and never getting out. The speed and power of the game were overwhelming. I also had a bad case of home-sickness. I was missing my mom as much as ever. Living at home through college kept her memory close. Now I was sleeping on a borrowed bed in a dorm two thousand miles from home, asking myself why I would go through another day of getting my chest caved in.

If I had left training camp right then, people would have understood. I didn't have to mention my ribs. My mother's death was reason enough. Many players were raised by single moms; losing a mother was like being orphaned.

I wrestled with my emotions all night. It was the darkest time of my young life. I knew my mom would want me to stay. Had she been able to speak to me in that difficult moment, she would have reminded me of how hard I had worked and how my dream was not yet complete. *Find a way to stay,* she would have said.

It took much more than positive attitude to suit up that next morning. But as I walked to practice, I reflected on the first time I saw a football game on television. I remembered how badly I wanted to play and how that desire had never diminished. Suddenly I was that kid again and I was wearing the uniform of a team I idolized. I was living my dream.

I peered up the ramp at the field glowing in the morning light. I played on that field. I inhaled slowly, held my breath, and pressed my fingers against my ribs. Pain. It was only pain.

I then exhaled a new level of nasty.

Nothing would stand in my way—not my ribs, not another player, not the intensity or intricacies of the game. I marched onto the field and tried to break every bone that crossed my path.

I quickly learned this is the only way a rookie earns a job. The intensity in training camp is junglelike. There is nothing like it in all of sports. Giant men with mortgages to pay, families to feed, and dreams to fulfill are pitted against twenty-two-year-olds trying to put them on the streets. I had to fight my guts out every play. I also made it my one goal to make no mental errors. I had to find a way to set myself apart from the other rookies; nine were drafted ahead of me.

I prepared myself well. The corkboard where I first tacked "FIND A WAY" had been my personal playbook in the weeks leading up to training camp. I had jotted every play on a note card and pinned them to the board in specific categories: screens, strong-side runs, weak-side runs, and passing plays according to the depth of the quarterback's drop. Every night before I went to bed and every morning when I woke up I voiced the plays aloud and rehearsed my assignment. It paid off.

Through five weeks of training camp I made only one mental error. Instead of running a flat route, I ran a flare. On my way back to the huddle, Noll turned to Coach Hoak and muttered, "I thought you said he was smart."

It was Noll's way of saying, "I've been watching you. I know it's your first mistake. Now show me how you respond."

Coach Noll was famous for testing players. He was always observing, always waiting to see how you'd do when things didn't go your way. He understood that thriving in the NFL took far more than optimism. It took wisdom, guts, and constant resolve. He made sure his teams possessed all three from day one. There were subtle ways of doing this and there were not-so-subtle ways.

One of Noll's few spoken rules was that if you were hurt, you had to stay away from the team. He didn't want you on the field or anywhere near the practice. Out of sight, out of mind was the point.

The same week I made my first mental error, another running back who was hurt had been standing around in practice. The running backs had been working with our position coach, which had allowed this other back to stay off Chuck's radar. But then he came over to work with us. You had mixed feelings when Chuck worked a drill because he was such a great teacher, but he was also very intimidating and the intensity always went to another level. You wanted to be on your best game. Chuck began instructing us and then we started in on a run drill. The hurt running back walked closer to the other players to watch. I understood why—he wanted to learn what we were doing. But he was on thin ice.

Chuck saw him and yelled at him to get back.

The player stepped back a few feet.

I could see Chuck was not satisfied. "Get out of here," he yelled.

The player backed up even farther. It was not enough.

"No," asserted Chuck. "Get out of here, as in off the field and out of here. Meaning, off the team."

Two people came up and escorted the guy off the field and to the front office. We went back to work. An hour later, we saw a van driving him to the airport.

Pads popped in practice that day as they never had before.

The NFL is a place where dreams are satisfied and shattered every day. Many make it there but never step onto the field during a real game. Their dream is nothing like they imagined.

Others have a flicker of glory but fail to find the fire again. They have only a brief taste of their dream. Most are forced into early retirement from either emotional or physical injury—often both. Such players often suffer well beyond the NFL because they never find the link between gutsy, unwavering action and achievement. They try again and again to hope and hype their way to victory.

According to the NFL Players Association, the average career span of an NFL player is only three and a half seasons, or approximately 56 games.[2] It took far more than a smiley disposition for me to play in 117 straight games with broken bones and torn ligaments against fierce linebackers like Mike Singletary and Lawrence Taylor.

You've probably heard it said that attitude gives you altitude. That trite notion doesn't work in the world of professional football. The NFL doesn't reward attitude. It rewards results. Chuck Noll knew how to get them.

Uncommon Effort

The Steelers were playing in RFK Stadium for my first preseason game and I was made the starting upback on the punt team. It was a big responsibility and a good indicator that the coaches thought I had a chance to make the team. I was essentially the quarterback on the punt team. I set the protection and the direction of the kick and gave the signal to snap the ball. I was also the personal protector for the punter. If a Redskins player broke through, I kept him from blocking the kick.

My first opportunity arrived shortly into the game. I jogged onto the field and took my place between the long snapper and punter about seven yards behind the line of scrimmage. Our line came set and I barked out the call. The ball was snapped to our punter and every Redskin turned around and ran to set up a return. With no one to block, I shot out of a cannon downfield and had the first shot at the returner.

But the guy was a water bug. He made one move, and I

grabbed air and went flying to the ground. He zigzagged from one side of the field to the other and I jumped up and locked my sights on him again. He had embarrassed me. He hopped and slid through our team, looking for an upfield seam. I sprinted straight ahead like a missile to the back of his jersey. He burst into a clearing. Just then I crashed down on him like a lion on the back of its prey.

I tried to break him in half.

When I arrived for the special teams meeting the following morning I was surprised to see Coach Noll standing at the front of the room. Normally our special teams coach ran the meeting. Once all the players settled in, Noll signaled for somebody to turn off the lights. He then picked up a red laser pointed and started the tape.

"I want you all to watch this," he said as he rested the red laser dot on me in my upback position.

Great, I thought to myself. *I'm dead.*

The ball was snapped and punted and Noll followed me with the red dot as I sprinted down the field. Just before the returner caught the ball, he paused the tape. He kept the lights off and the red dot pointed at me.

"Why is Merril ahead of everybody?" he said to the dark room. "He should never be the first one down the field."

He started the tape again and followed me with the red dot as I missed the tackle.

I cringed. I knew a reprimand was coming.

He said nothing and only left the red dot where I had gone tumbling out of the screen.

"Watch this," Noll then said.

I reemerged on the screen where Chuck's dot was waiting and he followed me all the way until I made the tackle. He stopped the tape and told somebody to flip on the lights.

He looked around the room.

"If you want to make this team," he asserted, "then give me *that* kind of effort every time you take the football field. Merril did that on every play he was out there and we need everyone to do that."

He then told us a story.

"When Donnie Shell came to the Steelers as a free agent, he couldn't catch a ball if I lobbed it to him. Do you know where he was a half hour before practice every day? With the receivers catching balls. Do you know where he was after practice every day? Catching balls from the machine. He used to put that machine on high and he practiced until he turned a weakness into a strength. Now he holds the record for the most interceptions by a defensive back in Super Bowl history."

He looked around with that famous glare.

"Every one of you, if you're good at something, that's all you do. Everybody works on their strengths, but it takes great desire and discipline to work on the things you're not good at."

His point was clear.

I was worried he had given my secret away.

My worries compounded when at the very next practice everyone on special teams showed up early and stayed late. But with each succeeding practice, the numbers dwindled until, two weeks later, the only people showing up early and staying late were those who had been doing it before Noll's speech. There were only a handful of us.

In the end of the matter, I dropped the worries and realized I had finally done what I had been trying to do since the Steelers drafted me. I got noticed.

I would soon learn this was only one-half of the paradox of playing for Chuck Noll's Pittsburgh Steelers. On one hand, getting noticed was required if you wanted to play. On the other hand, getting noticed was required to be the last thing on your mind.

Before the Rooney family hired Chuck Noll to lead the Steelers in 1969, the franchise had hardly tasted victory. From 1933 to 1968, the Steelers managed only seven winning seasons and two postseason appearances in 1947 and 1963—both losses. Noll inherited this losing legacy and worked it off, leading the Steelers to progressively improving records of 1-13, 5-9, and 6-8 in his first three seasons.

By 1972 he had swung the franchise's momentum toward victory. Building a new legacy had begun. The Steelers finished atop the AFC Central Division with an 11-3 record and hosted the first ever playoff game at Three Rivers Stadium, a game they would win over John Madden's Oakland Raiders. While the Noll-led Steelers would go on to own the 1970s, winning four Super Bowls over a six-year span, Chuck Noll's legacy is best encapsulated by the one play that gave the Steelers their first-ever playoff victory.

Broadcaster Curt Gowdy called it an early Christmas gift. The play has since become more famously known in the catalogue of greatest NFL plays as the Immaculate Reception.

The date was December 23, 1972. Kenny Stabler had just scored on a thirty-yard scramble to put the Raiders on top 7–6 with only 1:17 left to play. Oakland's defense had been stifling all night long and nothing changed during the Steelers' final drive. With twenty-two seconds remaining, Madden's Raiders forced Pittsburgh into a fourth-and-ten from their own forty-yard line.

The play Noll called next, a 66 Circle Option to rookie receiver Barry Pearson, paled in significance to the preparation he instilled in his players prior to the ensuing moment. In fact, the play would come to matter only in the context of the opportunity it created for another rookie to display an attribute Chuck Noll expected from every player.

Terry Bradshaw barked the call and took the snap from Pro Bowl center Mike Webster. He dropped back, and pressure came immediately from Raiders linemen Tony Cline and Horace Jones. Bradshaw ducked a tackle and shuffled out of the collapsing pocket, where he planted and flung the ball from the Steelers twenty-nine to the Raiders thirty-five toward halfback John "Frenchy" Fuqua. Before Bradshaw's pass could land in Fuqua's arms, Raiders safety Jack Tatum delivered a crushing blow. The force of the hit sent Fuqua flopping to the ground and the ball flying backward into the air.

What happened next was outside the camera frame of the original broadcast.

If you were watching the game at home as I was, you saw only the collision and the football flying out of the bottom of the screen.

"And his pass is . . . broken up by Tatum," announced broadcaster Curt Gowdy. There was a pause in Gowdy's call as the camera remained on the site of Tatum's collision with Fuqua. Then out of nowhere Steelers rookie fullback Franco Harris came racing into the bottom of the screen. The ball was in his left arm.

"Franco Harris has it!" cried Gowdy.

By the time he and the viewing audience realized what happened, Harris was at the twenty-five and had only one man to beat. Harris straight-armed Raiders defensive back Jimmy Warren at the ten and crossed the goal line just inside the left pylon.

"And he's over!" shrieked Gowdy. "Franco Harris grabbed the ball on the deflection! Five seconds to go! He grabbed it with five seconds to go and scored!"[1]

Fans and players flooded the end zone.

The Steelers were miraculous 13–7 winners.

What many don't know is that without a specific trait Coach Noll required of all his players, the Immaculate Reception would not have happened. Noll called it "being uncommon."

Following the Steelers' victory, another camera angle showed Franco Harris running down the field full speed as Bradshaw released the ball. Harris's job on the play was to help in pass protection, but once Bradshaw began to scramble, he headed downfield to give the quarterback another target. When he saw Bradshaw's pass heading toward Fuqua, he sprinted to the ball looking to lay a block for his teammate. Over the years, many football fans—myself included—considered Harris's position on the field a fortunate accident.

I soon learned there was nothing accidental about it.

Days before the last preseason game, there was an article in the *Pittsburgh Post-Gazette* discussing the bubble players, the guys that had to play well in the game to have a shot at making the team. My name was on the list, but playing well didn't concern me. What did was that I was getting fewer reps in practice leading up to the game. We then played the New York Giants on a Saturday night and I did not play one down on offense. I played only on special teams. I remember thinking things did not look good for me.

After the game, Chuck laid out the schedule for next week and then left the locker room. We had the next day off, and then everyone on the team had to report on Monday. I knew the day off was so they could make final cuts.

I was staying at the downtown Pittsburgh Hilton, and when I got to my room that night around midnight I thought about the significance of the next day and decided not to set my alarm. I had no reason to get up early, and if someone called or knocked on my door and woke me up, that would not be a good sign.

I pulled the curtains and lay under the covers, hoping to wake up on my own.

I opened my eyes again at ten a.m. It had to be a good sign.

I flipped on the TV and the timing was uncanny. The local news was reviewing the list of players that had made the Steelers team.

I read that list quicker than I'd read anything in my life.

Then, there it was. My name. I had made the team.

I was so jacked up I called the Steelers' front office and asked for apartment recommendations. I then jumped in my car and went to find my home for my first year in the NFL.

The next day I went to work, a professional football player. I still had a lot to learn, and my first lesson would never leave me.

The 1987 preseason was over and we were preparing to play the mighty San Francisco 49ers in our first regular season game. Greats like Joe Montana, Jerry Rice, and Roger Craig were still there, and experts were picking them to win it all. We knew we'd have our hands full.

A few weeks earlier, Coach Noll had written a letter to all the players asserting it was time to return to the Steelers' old-fashioned, blue-collar style of play.[2] The 1980s had not been as good to the Steelers as the 1970s. Injuries plagued the team in 1980 and 1981. Then began the retirement years. Between the end of the 1981 season and the end of the 1984 season, Joe Greene, Jack Ham, Lynn Swann, Terry Bradshaw, Mel Blount, and Jack Lambert played their last NFL games. While the team earned playoff births in three of those four years, the bunched departure of the team's leaders initiated a rebuilding phase. "It's not pleasant when you lose your whole football team," Noll famously told a reporter during that period.

In 1985 and 1986, the Steelers did not finish above .500 for the first time since 1971. By my rookie season in 1987, Coach Noll was poised to turn the tide again as he had done nearly twenty years earlier. As we prepared to play the 49ers, he was particularly intense about every player meeting the high expectations of the Steelers' legacy.

During practice one day, our quarterback, Mark Malone, called a pass play from the huddle. I was in at fullback and my assignment was to check the outside linebacker. If he rushed, I would block him. If he didn't rush, I would run a flat route.

Malone stepped to the line, barked the call, and took the snap. My linebacker dropped into coverage and I ran a flat route. Malone threw the ball to the other side of the field, and Louis Lipps pulled it in and turned to run. A quick whistle blew.

"Merril," yelled Coach Noll, "what are you doing?"

I hadn't learned everything, but I'd been through six weeks of training camp and preseason, and I did know that Noll never asked what you were doing if you were doing something right. I swung my head to look for the linebacker, thinking he must have blitzed after I started running my route. He hadn't.

I turned back toward Chuck.

"Nothing," I yelled back.

Noll then pointed to Lipps and glared at me.

"I can get anyone out of the stands to check the outside backer, run a flat route, and do nothing, Merril."

As my embarrassment rose he continued:

"How do you know Louis won't fumble and you could recover? How do you know he won't break a tackle and you could make the key block to spring him for a touchdown? I know

71

one thing—you can't do either of those things standing way over there doing nothing.

"Merril, I did not keep you on this football team to be a common football player. I need you to be uncommon, and the only way you can do that is to show up no matter where the football ends up. Fly to the ball when your assignment is complete. That is how you become uncommon and become as great a player as you can be."

It was a humbling lesson I never forgot because the first thing that came to mind was the Immaculate Reception. I realized right then that if Franco Harris had been a common player, the play would not have concluded the way it did. Had Franco not flown to the ball at full speed, had he been merely jogging or standing there watching the pass, he would never have been in position to make that unforgettable shoestring catch.

In that moment I learned the difference between running down a punt returner who made you miss and running to help your teammate thirty yards down the field.

Chuck Noll, the man whose first NFL draft pick was Mean Joe Greene, built the Steelers' legacy on this principle of being uncommon. Finish every drill. Run through every play whether or not you have the ball. Play as if every play can make or break the game—because it can. Being uncommon had many manifestations in Noll's steely eyes: tenacity, resolve, and resilience, to name the obvious. But the surest and subtlest embodiment of uncommon play was selflessness.

To fly to the ball full speed when the play is twenty, thirty, even forty yards downfield took absolute selflessness. You had to be thinking of your teammates in those moments, not personal pride, safety, or statistics.

It didn't matter who you were—in Noll's system you were expected to think of the team at every moment. When each player embodied such selflessness, it not only changed the outcome of games, it forever altered the attitude of an organization. Both occurred in Pittsburgh because the trait trickled down from the head and washed over every player. It especially oozed from the coaches and players who had been with Noll from the beginning.

I remember an instance in a game against Kansas City early in my career. We were on about the Chiefs' forty-yard line, and it was third and long. Bubby Brister snapped the ball and the defense got to him immediately. To avoid the sack, he dumped the ball off to me. I was like a magnet. Five defenders instantly converged on me. I had fourteen yards to the first and getting there would be a struggle.

I gritted my teeth and put my head down. I broke one tackle and then another. As I approached the marker, two more defenders draped on me. I kept fighting upfield as the defenders pulled me toward our sideline. I stretched out the ball as I lunged for the first down. I then looked up from my stomach and saw I was a yard short.

I took a deep breath and was about to push myself up when I felt an enormous hand come down on my back and lift me to my feet. I turned and saw it was Mean Joe Greene, who was then an assistant coach with the Steelers.

He pulled my face mask to his face. "That kind of effort," he asserted, "is the difference between a punt and a field goal."

The next play, Gary Anderson put three points on the board in a game we would go on to win by six. It was a memorable illustration of the common phrase that football is a game of inches. What many overlook is that those extra inches are won or lost on every down by the combined efforts of every player on a team. In this context, it is not difficult to understand why teaching players to be uncommon was so critical to Coach Noll. And the lesson reached well beyond the game.

To outsiders, Chuck appeared cold and emotionless toward his teams as he paced the sidelines in silence and glares. The truth was quite the opposite. Noll cared so deeply for each player that he paid no mind to personal accolades. He was as quick to take the blame for a loss as he was to pass the credit for a victory. He was famous for deflecting praise to "the guys"—the players who won the game on the field. Perhaps the subtlest testament to Noll's selflessness was the fact that he was the only coach of his time without a radio or television show.[3] Players mattered, not personal publicity.

Noll's secret was that he saw himself first and foremost as a teacher of men, not the king of a court. His preferred method of coaching was one-on-one instruction after practice. He spent countless after hours with players honing skills and perfecting basic techniques. For this reason, his highest ideal of success was not victory but maximum effort. "A life of frustration is inevitable," he once told a reporter, "for any coach whose main enjoyment is winning."[4]

It didn't take long for me to realize Chuck Noll's leadership was extraordinary. He, more than anyone, helped me pave the path to becoming not only the best football player I could be, but also the best person. In my rookie year there were more moments than I can count in which his confident persistence taught me as much about winning the game as being a winner in life.

Noll never seemed surprised by my mistakes. While he always let me know my errors in a way only he could, he moved quickly from telling to teaching. At the college level, technical mistakes tend to be less costly. A bigger, better team can overcome a mistake-filled game to a point. At the professional level, the gap between the worst and best is much smaller. One misstep, one blown coverage, or one lean in the wrong direction can kill a play or, worse, surrender the momentum of a game. This is why you always hear analysts, coaches, and players explain that when two equally matched teams play, the team with least mistakes usually wins. These mistakes are not just the obvious poor passes, mishandled snaps, and missed tackles. They are also the subtle technical details of every block, every pattern, and every pursuit angle.

I spent numerous hours before and after practice working with Chuck and Coach Hoak on technical tendencies I needed to improve. One in particular was my tendency to be impatient.

I was the third-down back during my rookie year. Most would agree that third down is the most critical down in football. But if it's not the most critical, it's certainly the most tense. Third and short is a vicious street brawl, hand-to-hand combat over a few feet of soil. Third and long is a violent bull rush that is either contained or comes crashing down. In either situation, one technical mistake can mean the end of somebody's day, year, or career.

It was midway into the season and we faced a third and six from our opponent's thirty-yard line. Everybody in the entire stadium knew the defense was going to open the gates and send the bulls. I didn't mind. I was good at reading blitzes, even in my rookie season. I loved blocking on third downs because it was like role reversal. Instead of being the guy others teed off on, I got to tee off on them. Sometimes I could even disguise my moves and earhole a guy so hard he would beg his coach not to blitz again.

But there was one problem. I had a tendency to be overly aggressive and get caught out of position. Sometimes I would get so caught up in determining who I was going to hit and exactly how hard I would hit him that I missed my block.

On this particular third and six, I was laser-focused on my target—an inside backer coming on a stunt blitz. As soon as Bubby snapped the ball, I attacked the spot where I knew he would come clean through the line. Back then, however, the game was so much quicker than I was used to. It was not uncommon for the whole playing field to go blurry on very chaotic plays. This was one of them. Two seconds after the snap, the backer disappeared from my sight.

A split second later I heard a collective groan from our home crowd. I turned around and saw Bubby peeling himself off the grass. The defender who sacked him was celebrating. I wondered where the guy came from.

As Bubby got some help up I looked to the sideline. Chuck was pointing at me with his index finger rolling toward himself. Not a good sign.

I was hoping he wanted my take on which idiot had just gotten our quarterback killed. It turns out I was partially right. He definitely wanted to discuss the idiot: me.

"What are you doing?" he demanded. "The guy ran right by you and killed Bubby!"

I have to admit that had there been a stack of Bibles, I would have slapped my hand on them and sworn the guy he was talking about was not the guy I was responsible for. I listened to Noll's vent, accepted it humbly, and sat on the bench—but I knew he was dead wrong.

"The eye in the sky never lies" was a common phrase heard during films. We reviewed each play from two different angles: once from the sideline angle we called the "all 22" because you could see every move by all twenty-two players on the field, and again from the end zone angle. What might have been missed in the game was no longer hidden in films. The eye in the sky revealed the truth about every play. I just knew the eye would prove my case. I went into films on Monday morning ready to accept Chuck's and Dick's apologies and move on.

The tape rolled and finally came to the play where Bubby got blown up. I watched carefully and there was absolutely no doubt. The guy who blindsided Bubby didn't just run by me, I might as well have high-fived him on his way.

Embarrassment doesn't describe how I felt. I was mortified. I wanted to fall through the crack of my chair.

Chuck had me come to practice early the next morning. He met me on the field with Coach Hoak, and the two drew a giant L on the field. The side part of the L, Noll explained, represented the offensive line, and the bottom of the L was the line just outside and perpendicular to the tackle or tight end on my side. Chuck then explained that because I was five yards deep when the ball was snapped, I had time to react. I didn't need to attack any part of the L because if the defenders never crossed those two lines, they could not hit our quarterback. "But when someone does cross that L," Noll concluded, "attack him like you've been doing."

I immediately understood what the great John Wooden meant when he said, "Be quick but don't hurry." The simple lesson in patience made a profound impact on my inexperienced game. But it was merely one of many private lessons I received from Noll. It was the same for everyone privileged to play for him.

Chuck was always working with individual players before and after practice. He made it his primary business to know what each player was truly capable of. Such personal investment earned him the right to call you out when you were holding back or falling short. It also earned him the right to value traits many would overlook. Journalist Don Smith once noted,

When defensive end Dwaine Board was drafted in 1979 and he seemed likely to win a starting job, it meant Noll would have to cut veteran Dwight White. But Noll... could not bring himself to cut the veteran star. He never forgot the time White came out of the hospital,

30 pounds lighter, to play in Super Bowl IX against the Vikings.[5]

I witnessed this undying loyalty firsthand in the second-to-last game of my rookie season. We were playing the Houston Oilers at the Astrodome on December 20, 1987, for a game with major playoff implications. History was also coming into play. In an earlier meeting that season, the Oilers soured the rivalry with multiple cheap shots. Noll called out Oilers coach Jerry Glanville in a postgame press conference, and the league took undisclosed action against the Oilers for the extracurricular activity. When we traveled to the Astrodome for our second meeting, everyone expected the game to be hard-fought. But I don't think anyone expected it to get out of hand.

On a first down from the Oilers' twelve-yard line, Mark Malone handed the ball to Ernest Jackson, who ran over the right guard for a couple yards before he was swarmed and held up by Oilers defenders so others could do further damage. Jackson was finally slammed to his back, where he threw a punch at Houston defensive end Richard Byrd. Whistles blew and words were exchanged, but the fight didn't escalate beyond a harmless scuffle...until Glanville launched his missiles from the sideline. Two Oilers, Al Smith and Doug Smith, came rushing onto the field with orders to blow off steam.

Our fullback, Frank Pollard, was standing over Ernest Jackson when he saw the two Smiths coming. He turned and threw a shoulder into Al Smith, keeping him from doing damage, but Doug Smith, trailing a little behind his teammate, veered toward

Pollard's blind side and body-slammed him to the ground. The scuffle burst into a bench-clearing brawl. When the dust and spit settled, six players were flagged for personal fouls, and three—Richard Byrd, Doug Smith, and Frank Pollard—were ejected.

Fights happened in the heat of battle and Noll understood that well. But he firmly believed they should be settled by the players on the field. He despised a coach sending mediators from the sideline to clean up a mess. Glanville had broken a cardinal rule this time, and Noll meant to tell him.

After the game, I happened to be walking next to Noll as he approached Glanville. I could see Chuck was boiling mad. I'd never seen a scowl quite like that one. He marched up to Glanville and grabbed his hand.

"You ever send one of your guys off the sideline after one of my guys on the field again, I will personally come to your side of the field and find you."

Glanville looked as if he'd been sucker-punched. He just stared sheepishly and then turned to walk away.

Chuck kept hold of his hand. He pulled him in closer. "I'm serious!" he fumed with a finger in Glanville's face. "You get it?"

The media would play up the incident and Glanville would gladly add fuel to the fire. He loved the attention. Chuck was different. He refused to talk about it in public. It was a different story in the locker room after the game.

He looked at us like a father to his sons, passion beaming from his eyes, and commanded, "No one will ever leave the sideline to fight. But if we are ever on the field and something like that breaks out again, you protect each other. As long as you do that and don't start it, I will pay your fines."

After hearing that, there wasn't a wall I wouldn't run through for Chuck.

Noll relished watching his players become the best they could be for the benefit of the team. He was paternally strict and expected every one of us, from the superstar to the practice squad sub, to display rugged passion, personal responsibility, and a disregard for personal accolades. But what set Chuck apart was that his high expectations were paired with exceptional patience. He seemed to always know the difference between a player with issues he could not overcome and one who would work hard until he got it right. I was the latter, and he was discerning enough to wait for me to develop.

It was extremely good fortune to come into the league as a Steelers player under a coach as discerning as Chuck Noll. My first season was fraught with lessons—some coming on the heels of frustration and failure, others on the heels of pure embarrassment.

In early November, I had just finished practice and was sitting at my locker when Pat Hanlon, one of our PR directors, came up to me and asked if I would speak at a midget banquet for Craig Wolfley. My first reaction was surprise that Wolf had gotten hurt. He looked fine in practice. I would later learn some veterans agree to do engagements over the summer when it seems like a good idea but then, when late October or early November hit, they wonder why they would ever commit to drive an hour after practice on a Friday. I didn't know this system yet.

Pat Hanlon is one of those guys who could sell ice to an Eskimo, but this opportunity did not require a sales job because my next thought was, *Wow, midgets playing football—good for them!*

After receiving directions, I raced home, changed, and headed back out. I had an hour's drive to put together my thoughts for the speech. As I headed down the highway, I started considering how I had been living in Pittsburgh for almost five months and had never seen a midget anywhere. It was odd, I thought, because to create a decent league you would need a minimum of forty-four midgets to form at least four teams, and even that would mean no backups and every player playing both ways. The more I thought about the numbers, the more I was inspired by their strength and will. I was honored to speak to them. They were not going to let a physical limitation keep them from playing this great game.

I got a little lost on my way, so I was late in arriving. Still, I was excited as I jumped out of the car and jogged into the building. I had never seen so many midgets gathered in one place, and I was hoping this would be a meaningful night for all of us.

As I entered the lobby, I noticed a lady sitting at what appeared to be the registration table. I quickly approached her.

"Is this where the midgets are having their banquet?" I asked.

She looked up and said, "You must be Merril Hoge."

"Yes, ma'am."

"Oh great—we've been waiting for you."

Then before I knew what hit me, she took my arm and whisked me onto a stage in a huge banquet hall and handed me the microphone. While the audience applauded, I had about ten seconds to scan the room and notice the huge banner in the back of the room that read: "Welcome Craig Wolfley." I also noticed the room was not full of midgets. It was full of little kids.

It then hit me. The banquet was for what we called Little League in Pocatello. I had never heard the term *midget* used in that same context. Suddenly, as I stood before some five hundred Little Leaguers and their parents, I was speechless. The only words I could muster were a confession.

I told them I did not realize the Midget League was the same thing as what I knew as Little League, and that I thought I was coming to speak to a room full of little people. As the laughter ensued, I then gave them the midget speech I had prepared in the car. Parents were on the floor and kids were crying with laughter, and we all had a great time at my expense.

There were moments like this during my first season in the NFL when it was painfully obvious I was both a rookie and a sheltered country boy.

I was adjusting to more than the way of the league and the quickness of the professional game. I was adapting to an entirely new way of life. Chuck was still willing to bet on my finding a way to succeed. Though he was fierce about winning games, he believed the greatest victories were won off the field. And he had an uncanny ability to know when they could be and had been won.

By the end of my rookie season, I had made strides. I began the season a rigid rule follower. I was focused on avoiding failure as much as securing success. One story testifies to the fact.

The team had some very strict rules on game days, especially in our locker room. The two big ones were "No strangers" and "No smoking." This was obviously on my mind as I sat in the locker room before our first regular season game against the 49ers. An older man walked in smoking a cigar.

My first reaction was to go over and speak to the guy and let him know he was not allowed in the locker room on a game day and especially not allowed to smoke. Rules were rules. But being a rookie, I said nothing and stayed in front of my locker and watched him walk around the locker room and wish everybody good luck, including me.

The next home game, the same thing happened. This time I had to do something. I didn't understand why no one was letting this guy know he was breaking the rules. As I thought about how to approach him to say something, I ran into equipment manager Tony Parisi. I asked him who the guy was and why nobody was saying anything to him.

"Have you ever looked at the bottom of your check?" Tony asked. "You should—you'll find his signature."

By the end of the 1987 season I had learned, among other things, what "the Chief" looked like and, more important, that Mr. Art Rooney enjoyed cigars whenever and wherever he pleased. Yet I had much more to learn and Coach Noll knew it.

It had been the year of the twenty-four-day players' strike, and I had played in only twelve regular season games. It was no wonder I received no props from Noll or any other coach when I went fishing for them in the locker room after the final game. I did, however, receive confirmation that I was growing in the right direction from a place I least expected it.

On my way out of the locker room, I was stopped by Dan Ferens, the chief contract negotiator. He was walking with the Chief.

The Chief looked at me and nodded. "You're one heck of a ball player," he said, then walked off.

Dan Ferens leaned in before rejoining him. "He doesn't say that to very many people."

I wanted my second season to begin right then. I knew deep down Chuck had seen something in me—perhaps something similar to what the Chief had seen—otherwise he would not have kept me on the team. I also knew that I hadn't accomplished much more than earning a job. It was more than some could say, but I still remembered the scout saying the Steelers needed me. I couldn't say it was true yet. The relationship was still more beneficial to me. I wanted to change that.

5

The Mind Fuels the Body

People like to discuss how the game gets more physical as you ascend the football ranks. The physical skills that earned you All-American honors won't ensure you excel in the NFL. You must get bigger, faster, and stronger. It's all true. But the mental advancement is more significant.

Professional football is the ultimate chess match. The players are pieces that must move with both physical strength and mental acuity. Brute strength can keep you in a game, but it alone will leave you vulnerable. And in the NFL, small advantages are the biggest difference between success and failure. Your physical strength and skills can be mitigated if one chink in your armor is exposed.

Anyone who has played in the NFL knows this to be true: physical skills fall short of potential without the fuel of the mind. I learned this lesson in my second year in the league.

Physical competence came naturally to me. The circumstances of my life leading up to the NFL prepared me to push my body to its limits. They also shaped strong emotional muscles. The sum of my life before the NFL was that I learned to be resourceful and optimize my physical skills. What I had not learned was the extent of my mental resources.

While my coaches perceived me to be a smart player, I had not yet learned to use the analytical intricacies of the game to my advantage. I was skilled but vulnerable. I have our bitter rivals, the Cleveland Browns, and specifically a veteran linebacker named Clay Matthews to thank for showing me how to take my game to the next level.

Matthews was a skilled and imposing physical presence, but he became a great player by learning to exploit every tendency and weakness in his competition. During our first game against the Browns in my second year, Matthews put this cerebral skill on display.

Each time we came to the line of scrimmage to execute a run, he started yelling out the play.

"Sweep! Sweep! Coming this way!" he screamed. Or "Trap! Trap! Going left!" And he was always right.

It was so uncanny that I started looking around during our huddle to make sure he wasn't listening in. It's hard enough to beat a team when they don't know the play, so you can imagine how hard it is when they do. We couldn't figure out how he was doing it. Had he found a copy of our playbook? Had he been around so long he just knew our offensive tendencies that well?

Our running game remained in this rut for nearly three quarters. We'd come to the line, Matthews would call out the play, and the Browns defense would stuff us. Then he made one blunder.

We called a sweep in the huddle and came to the line. Matthews immediately started yelling, "Sweep! Sweep!" Then he said the key words that gave away his secret: "Hoge is cheated up!"

A light went on as I realized he was predicting plays based on where I came set. He'd studied the game tape and noticed our backs' tendency to cheat up-and-out on sweeps and back-and-in on traps. We were trying to gain an advantage, but he turned this small detail into his team's advantage.

Our top rusher in that game, Ernest Jackson, had only 28 yards. I had 21. Our inability to move the ball on the ground was a primary reason Cleveland won.

That day I learned physical tenacity is not enough. Playbook knowledge is not enough. Even lucid execution is not enough. If your opponents know where you and the ball are going, you will rarely succeed. Against the greatest obstacles, you must find a way to stretch your mind to its potential.

This one lesson allowed me to catch up to the game much quicker than most young players. I became a straight-A student of the game. Memorizing plays and running them with precise execution and uncommon effort was no longer my highest standard. I studied film and sought small advantages on every play—even those in which I was physically overmatched. Instead of trying only to force my way to victory, I began to deploy a combination of force and acumen. I became a two-sided player. My game went to another level.

In the eighth game of my second season, I rushed for 94 yards and had 66 yards receiving against the Broncos. Noll gave me the game ball and anointed me the starter for the ninth game. It was my first career start.

I was amped to make a difference for the team.

Sometimes things don't work out as you plan.

While I got the start at fullback, I also remained on the punt team as the upback responsible for calling the punt plays. The combination ended up being a poor proving ground for my new-found mental tools.

I was so focused on perfecting my running plays and exploiting tendencies I had discovered in the New York Jets' defense, I forgot an important change we'd made in our punting scheme earlier that week.

We had some trouble that year getting punts blocked, so Chuck and our special teams coach decided to reverse the numbering system that indicated which defender each of us blocked. Until that ninth game, we numbered each defender from one to five, to the right and left of our center. The number five defenders were always the widest guys on the line to either side. Before the ball was snapped, my job was to make either a "Roger" or "Louie" call that would let our players know whether our center would block the number one defender to his right or left. The rest of us would then follow suit, picking up the rest of the defenders to ensure everyone was blocked. I always blocked the number five guy, who, in the old system, was the widest guy on the backside.

What had been switched before the Jets game was that instead of the numbering system beginning from our center at number one, it would begin at number five and count outward to one. This meant the widest defenders on either side of our center were now number ones.

I was so caught up in my first start at fullback, I remembered the new numbering system but forgot I was no longer blocking a number five defender.

On our first punt of the game, I made the call and the ball was snapped without incident. I then prepared to block a number five defender to the right of the center. As I stepped up to block him, I noticed he was already being blocked so I sprinted down-field. I didn't notice that the widest Jets defender on my side ran untouched to the punter. He barely missed blocking the kick. I got lucky that time.

We were up 10–3 in the second quarter when Malone threw me a pass in the flat. I turned back and was blinded by the sun. The ball hit my hands, bounced around my chest and shoulder pads, then hit the ground at our twenty-five-yard line. A former Steelers linebacker named Robin Cole scooped it up. I jogged over to him halfheartedly, knowing it was an incomplete pass. Then I saw the line judge signaling Jets' ball. I looked around in disbelief. It was called a fumble, and a few plays later Ken O'Brien threw a touchdown pass to Mickey Shuler to tie the score before half.

Normally this might be perceived as an unlucky break. Bad

call by the officials. After what happened next, however, it would only be thought of as part of a mental breakdown.

The Jets took a 17–10 lead in the third after a pass interference call on us put the ball at our one. After the ensuing kickoff, we moved the ball down the field and Gary Anderson made it a four-point game by the beginning of the fourth quarter. Our defense then stopped them from scoring and was poised to take back the lead. Unfortunately, we couldn't move the ball and lined up for another punt from our own twenty-nine-yard line. A good punt followed by a defensive stand, and we'd have the ball back with plenty of time to win the game.

Harry Newsome took his spot around the twenty and waited for the snap. I made the call and our center launched the ball to Harry, and again I went to block my number five guy next in the middle of the line. To my good fortune, he was being blocked again. I headed downfield.

I had taken no more than two steps when I heard a sound that still makes me sweat—the double-thud of the football bouncing off a punter's foot and then a defender's body.

The punt was blocked by a rookie defensive back named James Booty. Newsome scooped the ball back up at the seven but was immediately swarmed. Two plays later Freeman McNeil made it Jets 24–Steelers 13.

As I jogged off the field following the blocked punt, I could feel Noll's glare on me like the beating sun. I neared the sideline and saw his finger pointing at me and curling back toward him.

I approached in a cringe.

"You are the dumbest player I've ever seen!" he snapped. "How in the world could you make that same mistake again?"

He benched me for the rest of the fourth quarter. As I sat there I started to work out the numbers in my head. If Chuck had been coaching for about twenty-three years and if he had an average of eighty players each year, I was dumber than roughly 1,840 players. Not the kind of separation I was shooting for.

We subsequently lost the game and I went from game baller to goat in one week.

Chuck got straight to the point in the locker room.

"If Merril could count and catch we win this game," he said. "Now get showered and get dressed and let's get out of here."

I was never the MVP of any Super Bowl, but you would have thought so after that game. Chuck briefly answered the media's questions and then they swarmed me. I had reporters ten deep asking me how I could make the same mistake twice and whether I thought Noll was going to cut me.

With all the attention I was a little late getting cleaned up after the game. By the time I pulled off my pads and headed to the shower, I could hear water running from only one showerhead. I was relieved. I stepped into the open tiled space and my eyes met Chuck's. I felt more naked than I already was. He looked at me with suds still in his hair and walked out.

I stood under the water for about a minute and then quickly dressed and walked to the four buses always waiting for us after away games. My head was in a fog and I was ready to get out of there. I stepped onto the first bus and thought my luck was finally changing. The front row was empty. I plopped down and buried my head in my hands, anxious to put the worst day of my short NFL career behind me.

The day wasn't over yet.

A few minutes later, I lifted my head and saw Noll leaving the stadium. I started praying to my Father in heaven, "Please, please don't let him get on this bus."

As soon as I finished praying, Chuck made a turn toward my bus. I suddenly realized where I was sitting—but it was too late to do anything about it. Chuck had already stepped on board.

He stared at me sitting in his seat and I did the only thing I could think of. I scooted over.

Chuck grumbled something under his breath and then walked to the back of the bus, where he stood the entire ride to the airport.

Sports news coverage diagrammed my error the entire next week. The big question was: will Noll bench Hoge or cut Hoge? It was one or the other. Remaining a starter was out of the question.

Yet nothing changed.

Chuck said nothing more about it. He had a hunch the humiliation itself had solidified the lesson.

He was right.

I started at fullback the remainder of the year and played my mind and guts out. By the end of the season, I had amassed nearly

1,200 total yards from scrimmage with a 4.1 yard-per-carry average, 6 touchdowns, and a new franchise record for running backs with 50 receptions. I solidified a starting job, one I would never relinquish.

In my third year, Noll would begin holding me to his highest expectations. I was no longer the new kid. I no longer had the excuse of inexperience. It was time to put it all together. By average NFL standards, my career was already half over. The next two seasons would make or break me.

In 1989, I was so determined to be better than I had been the year before that I set my goals sky-high. I wanted to break my record for receptions and gain 1,000 yards receiving. To do so I needed to be in excellent shape.

In the off season I would get up at four-thirty a.m., drive to Three Rivers for a workout, eat breakfast, then drive to Washington & Jefferson College for a strenuous pool regimen with a seasoned trainer named Jack Rae. After the pool workout, I would eat lunch and then head to a martial arts class. This was my off-season routine five to six days a week. My body was totally depleted by the time I returned to my house each night.

While the routine greatly improved my strength and agility, I was overlooking a very critical element to sustained high performance: rest.

By the time training camp arrived, my body had been worn thin and it started to show.

While getting up at seven a.m. was like sleeping in, and

two-a-days were a cakewalk, my body was vulnerable. It needed a break I hadn't given it.

On the first day of training camp I pulled a hamstring. I tried to work through it and bruised my shoulder joint in the process. A couple days later, I aggravated my rib injury. I was a walking M.A.S.H. unit and it affected all aspects of my play. I was not hitting holes quickly. I was not running over defenders. I was sloppy catching the ball. I was a shell of myself and Noll knew it.

The receivers and backs were warming up with the quarterbacks one morning. As I jogged to the back of a line after catching a pass, Chuck was standing there, turned away and looking off into the distance. He started talking to himself but clearly loud enough for me to hear.

"They said to me, 'Do you think he is a flash in the pan?' and I said no way. But I guess I was wrong."

Chuck then walked away.

My blood boiled but I got the message loud and clear. Chuck did this often to see how players would respond to adversity.

In his own way he was challenging me to find a way to fix what was wrong. He believed in me and wanted me to succeed. There was never a doubt about this, and it made all the difference.

Noll was the greatest leader and teacher I've ever been around. His ability to motivate and maximize players was uncanny and unmatched. He seemed to always know the truth about a player. This knack was manifest in his development of young players, but perhaps more so in his unparalleled selection of college talent. He was responsible for drafting ten future Hall of Famers—Greene, Bradshaw, Blount, Ham, Harris, Lambert, Webster, Swann, Stallworth, and Woodson. He selected four of the ten Hall of Famers—Lambert, Webster, Swann, and Stallworth—in the first half of the 1974 draft. Such a feat has never been duplicated.

One of the greatest lessons I learned from Noll is that there is always more to learn. There is always room for growth. The moment a player thinks he has arrived is his moment of demise. It is a difficult lesson for many NFL players, because most opportunities for growth come on the heels of frustration or failure. But if you can't learn from adversity, your career will be short-lived. Your skills will stagnate, and someone younger and hungrier will be waiting to take your place.

Professional football, and all of life for that matter, is a path strewn with far more mistakes than masterpieces. The more battles you face, the more you comprehend that the one who learns to thrive amidst pain, frustration, and failure is the common victor. And this takes as much mental fortitude as physical grit.

This is the player and person Chuck taught me to become.

I came to the Steelers at the beginning of a rebuilding process. They won four Super Bowls the decade before, but the only remnants of that era were Mike Webster, Donnie Shell, and John Stallworth. We were a young and inexperienced team. To make any strides, we had to learn to fight from our backs. There was skill and intellect involved. Chuck taught us how, and my third season, 1989, was a Cinderella year for the Steelers.

97

Outside the front office and locker room, few believed we would accomplish much. We finished under .500 the previous year, and opened the season by getting trounced 51–0 at home by the Browns. We fared no better in our second game, getting hammered 41–10 by the Cincinnati Bengals. Bubby Brister and I shared a row on the bus ride to our plane after the game. As the bus pulled from Riverfront Stadium, we looked at each other and nodded. We officially stunk.

When you lose two games like that in the NFL, you get attacked by everyone and from every angle. People were saying we were the worst Steelers team in recent memory. To make matters worse, the Minnesota Vikings were coming to town the following week, and they were 2-0.

I don't know how many doormats beaten 91–10 in the first two games of the season have gone on to make the playoffs, but that's what Noll expected of us. He did not overreact. He was not happy, but I'll never forget what he said the week after our second blowout loss in a row.

He stood before us in our team meeting room as we prepared for our first full pads practice of the week. The first words from his mouth were, "Men, I believe in you." He went on to explain it would not be easy, but if we listened to him and followed the coaches' game plan for each game, we could right the ship.

No one outside our locker room thought we could win. Still, we played the next game against the Vikings with extra grit and energy, and won. The next day I woke up to a big spread in the

Post-Gazette trashing me. I ended up leading the team in rushing that game, but the article attacked the coaches for letting me carry the ball more than Tim Worley, a first rounder out of Georgia. The writer of the article compared me to an AMC Gremlin and Worley to a Porsche. Why would you drive a Gremlin, the writer implied, when you have a Porsche in the garage? He clearly didn't understand the intricacies of the game and that our offensive plays were often dictated by how the Vikings were playing defense.

I cut out the article and used it to fuel my passion to keep fighting. Noll believed we could turn things around and so did I. We were only 1-2.

Sure enough, we did.

We won two of our next three games, including avenging our opening season 51–0 embarrassment with a 17–7 win in Cleveland. We won back our pride and then fought our way through the season. With four games remaining, we controlled our destiny. Chuck again stood before us in our team meeting.

"Win them all," he asserted, "and you will get into the playoffs." He said nothing more.

We lost the first of those final four games at home to Glanville's Oilers. It was a tough loss, especially given the history of the two teams, but Noll maintained his belief in us. We ran the table in our final three games and with some help made the playoffs and traveled to Glanville's self-proclaimed "House of Pain" for the Wildcard Game on New Year's Eve. There we upset the favored Oilers in overtime 26–23 and knocked them out of the playoffs.

I had one of the best games of my career: 100 yards rushing

on 17 carries and another 26 receiving. The longest run of my career set up an important field goal, and my 2-yard touchdown tied the game with forty-six seconds in regulation. It was the most physical game I ever played in. Bodies were flying and colliding with crushing force for sixty-plus minutes. There was no relenting on either side, and with every step on the Astrodome turf, I was utterly aware of being blown up.

I thought the game would never end. Then a couple of minutes into overtime Rod Woodson knocked the ball from the Oilers' Lorenzo White and pounced on it. Four plays later, we had our shot to end it.

My shoes sloshed and sweat dripped from my uniform as I walked to the sideline and took a knee. I could not fathom playing another down. I prayed we would make the field goal and, if not, that I'd somehow have the strength to move. Just then I looked up at the Astrodome big screen and read that the kick would be Anderson's first attempt at a fifty-yarder.

Gary has been around forever, I thought to myself, *and if he's never tried a fifty-yard field goal there is a reason—he can't make it!*

As my anxiety rose, I read the rest of the big screen. It was only Anderson's first attempt that season.

He split the uprights a moment later and the Astrodome fell silent—the sweet sound of victory on the road.

As we jogged across the field to the visitors' locker room situated behind the Oilers bench, I zeroed in on Glanville's ashen face atop his all-black attire. Noll didn't have to say a word. The Oilers coach was attending his own funeral.

Glanville was fired a week later.

We lost a heartbreaker at Mile High Stadium the following week when the great John Elway led the eventual AFC Champions on one of his famous fourth-quarter comebacks and a 24–23 win. Despite the loss, I was named the game's MVP and became only the second Steelers player in franchise history to rush for 100 yards or more in back-to-back playoff games (Franco was the first). I led our team with 120 yards rushing on 16 carries and another 60 yards receiving, but in the end it wasn't enough to keep the Bronco's Hall of Famer from working his last-second magic. After never leading in the game, Elway marched his team down the field on a seventy-one-yard drive capped by a one-yard run with 2:27 remaining.

After the game, the writer who had compared me to a Gremlin came up to me. "What kind of car are you?" he asked.

I looked him straight in the eye. "A Ferrari," I replied.

Mr. Rooney was behind the writer and I excused myself to greet him.

"I have never heard Chuck Noll talk so highly of a player as long as I have known him," he said.

It was one of the greatest compliments I ever received.

There is no doubt the loss was hard to swallow, but there are certain losses more meaningful than certain wins. Few had given us a shot to make it to five hundred that year, let alone make the playoffs and nearly upset the mighty Broncos, who had destroyed us 34–7 earlier that year. But Noll believed all along the way. We came to believe alongside him.

After the Denver game, a mechanical error delayed our departure for a couple of hours. We deplaned and sat back on the bus. I'll never forget the scene. It was calm and quiet except for soft jazz playing over the speakers. Everyone was keeping to himself. Chuck then stood up in the front of the bus and walked silently to the back, where he sat down and began educating us on great jazz music and the best places to hear it live. He talked jazz and cities and offbeat nightclubs where he once saw the greats play. For twenty minutes he continued without a word about the game. We listened and laughed and nodded with his stories. Then he stood up and returned to the front row as quietly as he had come.

I was amazed by his perspective.

While the final score of the game would sting for a long time, Chuck was always reminding us there were other important things in life. Following the Denver loss was no exception.

He would never say, "Hey, the loss is no big deal. Get over it. Now let's talk about jazz!" But after a loss, he would always subtly remind us there was more to life than football. To an outsider, the perspective might seem detached, even careless. It was quite the opposite to us.

Chuck Noll was bent on developing men, not mere athletes. Character, integrity, and leadership were more important to him than career statistics. He simply knew that when he turned a team of college boys into a team of mature men, success would come and continue long after the game. I don't think Chuck could look himself in the mirror—then or now—knowing he didn't prepare his players to be successful on and off the field.

As we flew home from Denver that night, what I thought of most was how the fans and media spent the entire season discussing how the game had passed Chuck by. It was time for him to do something else, they all said. He had led Pittsburgh to every Super Bowl the city had ever known. He turned a losing franchise into a legendary one. And people, as they always do, had short memories. They wanted somebody new.

In truth, the game hadn't passed Chuck by—he won his only NFL Coach of the Year award that year.[1] But perhaps Chuck had passed the game by. By the end of my third season, I think he knew he would coach for only a couple more years.

I like to think he stuck around a little while longer because there were lessons some of us still needed to learn.

They say there is nothing you can do to prepare yourself for cancer. While I understand the spirit of the statement, I believe if you were to look back on the circumstances of survivors' lives in the few years before the disease attacked, you would find moments that toughened their skin and trained their perspectives to beat the killer.

There is certainly no magic pill for defeating the disease—and unfortunately some cancers just won't quit. Still, those who beat it possess certain attributes that exponentially increase their chances to fight another day.

After the 1989 season, I was selected to the All-Madden Team and was recognized as the Steelers' Iron Man of the Year. I would win the Iron Man award again in 1990, after the statistically best season of my career, which included ten TDs and 1,114 yards from scrimmage. After four years in the league, I knew the real meaning of toughness. I had not missed a single practice or game. I had done everything Chuck asked of me. I had become an uncommon player—a combination of sharp skill and steely intellect, applied selflessly.

But such skill and intellect get you only so far. You eventually face greater battles than those already won. Only the individual with an iron will can continue to thrive.

So much of what someone is able to accomplish in life surrounds the X factor we call *willpower*. It is the one attribute we can least quantify. In fact, we can measure its existence or absence only in circumstantial context.

The uncommon achiever always finds new challenges. He is never satisfied to sit back and bathe in past success. His circumstances are always changing.

The common achiever quits while he's ahead. He seeks predictable circumstances he can control and maintain. He summits the mountain once and then descends to relish in his victory the rest of his life.

The problem is that progress is the shared gauge by which every person on the planet measures success. If the common achiever does not climb another mountain, the light of his previous victory will eventually dim. So too will his effectiveness. If disease or tragedy strikes at this vulnerable point, it is rarely a contest. Disease and tragedy are too strong. Even smaller opponents pose a major challenge when progress has stalled.

According to the World Health Organization, depression is the leading cause of disability in the world today. It is also projected to be, by 2020, the second leading cause of lost productive years of life due to premature death or disability.[2] There is a direct link between depression and progress.

If the tools that got you to the top of one mountain aren't tested on another mountain, and then another, you risk a greater loss than if you had never succeeded the first time.

A sad reality of the NFL is that more than three-quarters of all players are divorced, bankrupt, or unemployed two years after leaving the game.[3] The primary reason has little to do with mismanagement of money. It is an unwillingness to reallocate the tools that got them to the summit of football to new challenges after football. Most players don't have the will to ascend again.

Passion and the Prima Donna Syndrome

When I compare the final four years of my NFL career with my first four years, one distinction is clear. My effort didn't change, but the circumstances surrounding me did. New and unfamiliar mountains came into view and I had to make a choice: either ascend again or descend and relish in having lived out my dream.

I chose to ascend again.

I applied every bit as much skill and intellect in my final four years as I had the previous four. Yet the changing landscape of the game and my team required more than I had given before.

The average NFL career lasts only three and a half years. Breaking through that barrier became a question of skill, intellect, and a final ingredient called *will*.

While the 1991 season was a good one for me on the surface—nearly 1,000 yards from scrimmage—circumstances were changing beneath the surface that I could not control. Not only was Chuck concluding his Hall of Fame career and handing the coaching reins to Bill Cowher, the team had also drafted a powerful running back out of Arkansas named Barry Foster, and I was being asked to hand the rushing reins to him. My position was not being supplanted, but the game was changing my role.

In the early 1990s, the NFL was becoming pass-happy. Offense-minded rule changes over the previous fifteen years opened the floodgates for receivers to become stars of the league. Coaches formed offenses like the West Coast and the Run-and-Shoot around robust, high-percentage passing attacks and multiple wide-receiver sets. In the first half of the 1990s, their plans started to pay off.

From the NFL's inception in 1920 through the 1989 season, only three players had reached the 100 receptions mark:

- Denver's Lionel Taylor in 1961 with 100
- Houston's Charley Hennigan in 1964 with 101
- Washington's Art Monk in 1984 with 106

Between 1990 and 1995, twelve players reached the mark:

- San Francisco's Jerry Rice with 100 in 1990, 112 in 1994, and 122 in 1995

- Houston's Haywood Jeffries with 100 in 1991
- Green Bay's Sterling Sharpe with 108 in 1992 and 112 in 1993
- Minnesota's Cris Carter with 122 in 1994 and 1995
- Atlanta's Terance Mathis with 111 in 1994
- Detroit's Herman Moore with 123 in 1995
- St. Louis's Isaac Bruce with 119 in 1995
- Dallas's Michael Irvin with 111 in 1995
- Detroit's Brett Perriman with 108 in 1995
- Atlanta's Eric Metcalf with 104 in 1995
- Green Bay's Robert Brooks with 102 in 1995
- Arizona's Larry Centers with 101 in 1995[1]

While the Steelers focused on maintaining a tough-nosed ground game in the midst of other teams' high-flying attacks, our offense still adapted. The change that most affected my role was transitioning from a split back formation to the I-formation. We ran it some in the final two years of Chuck's career, but when Cowher took over, it became the primary formation.

In the "I" the fullback is rarely a ball carrier. He is primarily a blocker for the tailback and occasionally a receiver out of the backfield. While I excelled at both tailback and fullback at Idaho State, I was known as a "tweener" in the NFL—neither fast enough to be a tailback nor big enough to be a fullback. A tweener fit well in Chuck's split back system. The fit wasn't so tight in the new system.

The role change would have been a far simpler task had all else remained the same. Instead of breaking bones with the ball in my hands, I would break bones as a blocker. But this became a difficult task, as the very ground on which I stood for the first four years of my career was also shifting.

There was a boiling undercurrent of legal proceedings between the league and the NFL Players Association that was changing the way players were paid and perceived. While the looming victory for unrestricted free agency would open the door for big dollars, it would also surface players' true means and motives of victory. The day of the pure player was dimming. The day of the prima donna was dawning.

Looking back, it is at least curious that Noll's final year in coaching corresponded with a change in the trajectory of the NFL and my NFL career. I don't know if there was a direct correlation between the new horizon and the dimming of Chuck's coaching days, but I do know that once his brilliant career came to a close, I found myself amidst circumstances that demanded I tap my deepest passion to play the game. That passion fueled my will.

What happened during the fourth game of Chuck's last season is probably more symbolic than directly sent by God to prepare me for my changing circumstances. Yet in either context it served as a primer for the intangible battles I would fight in the final three years of my career.

We were playing the Eagles in Philly, and that year they had one of the greatest defenses of all time. Defensive ends Reggie White and Clyde Simmons would amass 28 sacks between them, Jerome Brown would tally an unheard-of 9 sacks from the defensive tackle position, and Seth Joyner would add another 6.5 sacks from inside linebacker. All told, nearly half of their starting defensive unit (five players) would go to the Pro Bowl that year. They were big, strong fighters who played the game with an intense passion.

I knew the game was going to be different than most based solely on how the day began. Two hours before game time, I jogged through the visitors' tunnel and onto the field for an early pregame warm-up with wide receiver Jeff Graham. Very few players were on the field, and Veterans Stadium was mostly vacant except for the avid fans who must have camped out at the gates the night before.

As we approached the spot where we planned to stretch, I noticed a Philly fan trailing us along the railing a few feet above us. I thought it was odd but didn't pay him much attention until we stopped and started to stretch. Out of nowhere the guy started giving me a tongue-lashing so bad it would make a sailor cover his ears. He called me vulgar names I had never even heard, and he made sure I knew how terrible a football player I was.

Graham and I finished our stationary stretches and went into a series of lunges and sidesteps up and down the sideline. The fan shadowed us back and forth along the railing, hopping over stairs and seats as necessary, screaming obscenities all along the way. We had ignored him to this point, but his rant went on so long and so loud that finally Jeff Graham started to laugh. I'm not joking when I say that the guy could have won a contest for the longest tirade in history.

Finally his anger reached a head and the source of his rage was revealed.

"You're an idiot!" he screamed. "You fumbled in my Tecmo Bowl championship and I lost!"

Tecmo Bowl was the first successful NFL-themed video game, and I was a beast on it. Coach Madden rated the players and he gave me a high rating for being physical and tough. I could almost not be tackled. I used to have Tecmo Bowl Mondays at my house with guys on the team, and of course I would play myself. One thing I learned, however, is that while my video self could pile up the yards and points, if you hit the C button too many times, making me spin, I would fumble.

After recovering from astonishment that a video game could actually infuriate someone to that level, I laughed and then yelled back to the guy, "Stop hitting the C button too much!"

He had nothing else to say and we finished our warm-up in peace.

The incident was only the beginning of a day that seemed to surround a deep and personally affecting lesson in thick skin.

If you play in the NFL long enough, you get your shots and take your shots just the same. This is one of the games within the game that plays out between two opposing players whose paths collide often throughout their sixty minutes together. To win this game within the game is simple—give more shots than you receive by the end of the game. But occasionally the battle doesn't end when the clock hits zeros.

My second birthday in the kitchen of my childhood home in Idaho.

My sun-stained face from my afternoon paper route in fifth grade.

My brothers and I call this our team photo. From left to right, that's Marty, Chris, me, and Rick, the oldest.

Team McDonalds, sponsored by the local golden arches. I was in middle school and wore number eleven.

Running the ball as a junior at Idaho State in a game against our arch rivals Boise State.

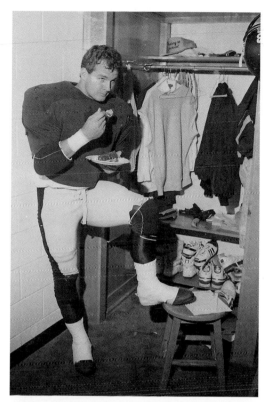

Eating cheesecake in front of my Steelers locker. A Friday, post-practice tradition courtesy of local Pittsburgh proprietor, Rick McMaster.

After knocking Jerry Glanville's Houston Oilers from the 1989 play-offs, Bubby Brister points a heckling Oilers fan to the scoreboard while Monte Dawson and I look on.

My first 100-yard game. I would have seen the end zone, if it wasn't for Reggie White (number 92).

Getting ready to engage in battle, you can tell by my eyes.

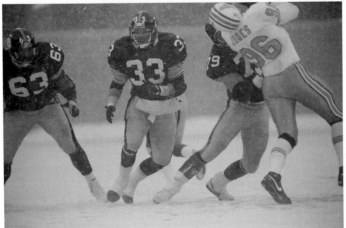

When I was a kid, I dreamed of playing in weather like this. Not much changed after I made it to the NFL.

The finishing touches to a successful drive against Denver during the playoffs in 1989. We had a play designed specifically for Denver's defense, and it worked like a charm.

The first action shot of me in a Bears jersey.

The last helmet I ever wore. The hit that ended my career crushed the steel facemask like it was made of wicker.

Me with Steelers broadcasting legends Myron Cope and Bill Hill-grove. Their faces don't show how much they had to put up with me that year.

My second family at ESPN during my first year on the *NFL Matchup* show. In the striped shirt is the show's producer, Greg Cosell.

The last Chicago Bears game of the 1994 season. I brought my camera and Walter happened to be there.

Hines Ward, Mark Bruener, Carnell Lake, and me after the annual Hoge-Ward Celebrity Golf Tournament to benefit the Highmark Caring Foundation.

My younger brother Marty and me with the great Chuck Noll after the golf tournament.

My angel Kori and me horse-back riding in the mountains near our Idaho cabin.

My stud Beau and me having fun on a buddy day.

Me, Beau, and Kori on a family hike (mom is behind the camera) at the Continental Divide about a half hour from our cabin.

Once the game against Philly started, it quickly became clear that a linebacker named Seth Joyner and I were going to continue a battle that began the year before. We were playing in Pittsburgh. I caught the ball out of the backfield and turned upfield along the Eagles sideline. He came barreling in on me and I put my shoulder down and ran him over. Nothing is more embarrassing in football than getting trucked in front of your own teammates. While it happens to everyone, Joyner was a big, physical linebacker and it didn't happen to him often, if ever before then. I knew he was not happy about it.

Now we were playing on his home turf in Philly and early in the game, like déjà vu, I caught a pass out of the backfield again and turned upfield near the Eagles' sideline. Joyner flew over to hit me just like the year before. Again, I gave him the same-foot/same-shoulder technique Chuck taught us. With my hips and back straight, I bent my left knee so that my quad was parallel to the ground and coiled like a spring. When Joyner arrived, I struck him with my left forearm and simultaneously sprung my body upward into his body with a rising blow, lifting him into a helpless position. Again, I trucked him in front of his teammates.

I don't know if the hit jogged Joyner's memory or he was just having a bad day, but this time he didn't go away quietly. He jumped up and gave me a cheap shot to the stomach. I exploded and went at him, and fists started flying and mouths started running. Just as I was about to get my hands on him, I was completely immobilized. Someone grabbed me from behind and took me to the ground, and the only muscle I could move was my mouth.

I yelled at whoever it was to get off me, and Joyner yelled at me while the officials held him back. Things started to calm down and I was allowed to move again. As I stood up, blood still boiling, I met my captor. It was Reggie White. I played against him three or four times in my career, and although I never fought a real grizzly bear, I swear I now know how it would be. I never, before or after, played against someone with such incredible power and strength.

After having been pinned by Reggie, I had a different understanding of Joyner that I intended to make known. As we walked back to the huddle we kept jawing at one another.

"I'd run my mouth too if I had Reggie to protect me!" I yelled.

Seth blew his lid and the game was on all day.

While I was never an instigator or a cheap-shot artist, I was also not one to back down, in word nor deed. The battle raged between Joyner and me nearly every offensive play. The more he talked, the better I played, and the hotter the battle blazed.

We were whipping the Eagles' backsides in the first half, but something changed in the second. Reggie went to another level and took the game onto his broad shoulders. Our offense sputtered through the third and fourth quarters, and Philly eventually tied the game. With the swing in momentum, Joyner's mouth swelled. So did mine.

Our battle finally boiled over.

Our offense failed miserably on first and second down during one of our last drives. It was third and long, and Chuck called a draw play to try and catch the Philly defense off guard.

I had a bad feeling as we broke the huddle.

The feeling was confirmed when we snapped the ball.

Bubby went into his drop and I watched Reggie White, Jerome Brown, and Seth Joyner breaking through our line and converging in my direction. I stood my ground, not wanting to give the play away, but it was quickly becoming clear that didn't matter.

As Bubby slipped me the ball, two things were certain: a first down was out of the question, and gaining even an inch was unlikely.

A third thing was also certain. I was going to make these dogs pay.

The one thought in my head was that if I was about to be pummeled behind the line, I was going down fighting. I would hit them as hard as I possibly could and make their hit cost them something. I squeezed the ball and targeted my nemesis, Joyner, knowing White and Brown would feel the collateral effects.

I took two steps and threw myself full force into Joyner and his giant battlemates. What happened next had never happened to me before.

The moment we collided I lost all control of my bodily functions.

I filled my pants like a one-year old.

It is hard enough playing the game when your pants aren't full, so you might imagine how hard it is to play even one snap when they are. I had half of the fourth quarter left to play.

After that series, I jogged to the sideline and asked my friend Tunch Ilkin to take a look at my backside.

"There's nothing there," he said.

I bent over and told him to look again.

"Oh my gosh!" he exclaimed. "You crapped your pants."

"No," I said, "I did not crap my pants—I got the crap knocked out of me."

There may be more truth than you know to someone saying a guy just got the crap knocked out of him. While I had some massive hits still coming to me, I fortunately never again fit that description so precisely.

They say the more things change, the more they stay the same. The adage seemed to encapsulate my fifth season in the NFL. The league was changing, my coach was changing, and my role was changing—but before it would all turn over, my circumstances briefly returned to the beginning.

Four games after the Philly mess, Barry Foster sprained his ankle and missed the next five games. I was given one last chance to carry the load like old times. I gave Chuck my very best.

In the off-season before my sixth season as a Steeler, Chuck Noll retired as quietly as a legend can possibly retire. I remember hearing the news and being shocked, even though I could feel something was different the last month of the 1991 season.

After his departure, there was an uneasy feeling about the

future of our team. We all felt it. We were still a young team, but there was an important distinction. We had been trained to play professional football by the best. All we needed now was the right marching orders and we would be fine.

The players had no clue who the next head coach would be but, in truth, I think we all felt sorry for him before we met him. How in the world do you fill Chuck Noll's shoes?

When the announcement was made that Bill Cowher was going to be our new head coach, I had mixed emotions. I initially wondered if he would come in and run everyone out of town, then go get guys he coached in Kansas City and Cleveland. It was quite the opposite. To his credit, Bill not only worked with the players we already had on the team, he intuitively recognized the strength of the team and built on that. He met with every player right away before we ever met as a team.

When he and I first met, he asked what I thought we needed to do differently as a team, and what personal goals I had for the next year and beyond. After I had shared, he took a turn sharing his goals for me personally, and for the team. I left the meeting excited to play for Bill Cowher. I believed he heard what I had to say and wanted to make changes that best motivated us as individuals and a team.

When Mr. Rooney formally introduced Cowher to the team for the first time, I was sitting in my normal chair to the left of the front and about five rows back. As he took the floor, I could see that he was shaking. Even his voice trembled a little. I remember thinking I would hate to be him. We had been led by a Hall of Famer and no matter what he said, he would have to prove it to us on the field. He knew it, too.

Bill stood before us and said, "I want you to understand one thing: my job is to get you ready for Sunday, and in order to do that we are not going to beat each other up Wednesday through Friday. We will practice with a quick tempo and we will hit, but I will take care of you during the week. Your job is to take care of me on Sunday."

It was immediately appealing to the players because one of the common comments Cowher heard in the individual meetings was that we often hit so much and so often in practice all week, by game time we were banged up and running on reserve. He had truly listened to us. But we all knew that saying something and doing something are two different things. Most of us were skeptical that Bill would not live up to his promise. He proved us wrong.

While that one change did not make him a great coach, it showed him trustworthy. Bill built on this foundation throughout the preseason as we worked hard to implement a new system. The real test, however, was our first game of the regular season. We were playing the Houston Oilers at their place. They had beaten us twice the year before and were widely thought to be the best team in our division and one of the best in the NFL.

During the week we had put in a fake punt and Bill had told us that if the game was close and we were at midfield, we would run it. Every coach puts in trick plays like this and says they are going to run them, and then they almost never do. So needless to say, we didn't think twice about the fake punt—until we had a fourth down around midfield in a close physical game.

I was jogging off the field when I heard the call.

I thought, *Are you kidding me? You're really going to run this?*

Again, I was proven the foolish skeptic. We executed the fake punt to perfection, and Warren Williams took the ball down inside the Oilers' five-yard line. One play later, we punched it in for a touchdown. That play on that day was a major turning point that not only won us the game, it won us over as players under our new head coach. Bill had done his part during the week. We had done ours on Sunday. It proved to be a successful combination that we never doubted again.

Playing for Chuck Noll was like playing for a brilliant father figure. Playing for Bill Cowher was like playing for an older brother you idolized. I would learn that while their styles were quite different, and while they offered me very different opportunities, both were great men whom I was privileged to call my coaches.

I would have loved for the conditions under which I came into the league to continue until my retirement, but I now know that change and adversity were my next great teachers. Chuck had always said he was preparing us for more than the game, and this preparation was coming due. While I would apply his life lessons under shifting conditions for another two full seasons, their real litmus test would come when nothing was the same. Not even my uniform.

Before that occurred, new conditions would stretch my resources and my resourcefulness. I had a new coach, which on a personal level was a smooth transition. On a professional level, it was a different story. Through a combination of changes in the game itself and an up-and-coming running back on the roster, blocking became my primary responsibility. I went at it the way I had always done, knowing that greatness is not bound up in numbers but rather in a player's ability to maximize all his God-given tools. Yet, contrary to years past, the feat took more than skill and intellect because not everyone on the new Steelers staff wanted me around.

Until my sixth season in 1992, I had never gotten caught up in team politics. That quickly changed when Cowher hired Ron Erhardt as his offensive coordinator.

Erhardt was a smart and successful offensive coach with a track record that included two Super Bowls with Bill Parcells's Giants. He was known primarily for his success with the running game—but despite my reputation with the Steelers, he had it out for me from the beginning. His wish list for the Steelers included ditching me and bringing in Maurice Carthon, his fullback with the Giants, who was then a free agent in his last year.

Where Chuck Noll had seen the upside of having a three-tooled back who could run, catch, and block, Erhardt wanted nothing to do with me. He wanted a prototypical blocking full-back like Carthon, who played like an extra offensive lineman. I was a contrast to the prototype. I used to sneak weights into my shorts just to weigh in at 220 pounds. The truth was that I played at 210 pounds, but the extra ten pounds was negligible. Erhardt had no use for a 210-pound or a 220-pound fullback who regularly ran and caught passes.

So Erhardt and I came to an understanding. I knew he thought I should disappear. He knew I thought he was wasting my talent.

In the end, however, he was calling the plays. While he couldn't cut me, he could limit my touches. I faced a choice every day. I could pout in a corner or pound away on every play whether or not Erhardt used me. I pounded away. The reason was simple.

I had to answer to myself first.

The question I always asked myself was whether I played the game as hard without the ball as I did with it. I knew it was one thing to turn on the talents when the spotlight is on you but entirely another thing to give the same effort when the lights are off. I have always been able to say I played with passion whether or not I had the ball, and whether or not I was anywhere near the play. This was later confirmed.

During Chuck's last two years, rumors swirled that the 49ers were interested in trading for me. They had Tom Rathman, who was a stud fullback in the NFL, but he was coming to the end of his career. The Niners were looking for a younger fullback to fill his shoes and complement Ricky Waters. After the 1993 season, Rathman left the Niners to sign with the Raiders, so I was invited to a meeting with George Seifert. It seemed everything was lining up perfectly.

The meeting started off well as we discussed our shared love of fishing. Then George directed our conversation to the real matter at hand.

"Merril," he said, "if this were the old days, I would just ask your price and you would give it to me and we would sign you right now. But right now we are only $100,000 under salary cap and can't even afford to run minicamp. So even though we want you to be a 49er, we are going to have to free up some money first before we can do that."

I was disheartened because I wasn't sure I could afford to wait a month or more to sign with a team. I didn't want to wait, have things change, and end up being left without a team. My next meeting with the Niners' running backs coach made the decision to not wait even tougher.

We sat down and he immediately complimented the way I played and how he loved that I could run and catch so well. However, what he said next blew me away.

"But what I love most about you, Merril," he said, "is how you play without the ball."

I asked him what he meant.

He explained how he went about evaluating a player. He would dim screen while watching tape, he said, and put a spotlight on one player so he could watch how he played on every play throughout the game—not just when he had the ball.

"I have seen very few in my career," he then confessed, "who play like they have the ball when they don't, like you do."

It was one of the best compliments I was ever given.

Still, not everyone shared the 49ers' sentiments about me.

Back in 1992, I was still a season and a half away from Erhardt's confidence reaching the same level. So in the meantime, he and I went at it nearly every day. While the team stretched, he would walk by and remind me that I was lucky the Rooneys liked me and Bill Cowher was in my corner, because "if not, you would be gone."

"If you're such a great coach," I would reply, "why don't you find a way to get the ball to a guy who gains 1,000 yards from scrimmage?"

He would make some derisive comment back to me and I would return it with a jab about how he must not know what to do with a fullback who could do more than block.

While Cowher did not tolerate players yelling at coaches—something I wholly agreed with—respect is always a two-way street, and I had remained Erhardt's doormat for too long without reprieve. The war of words began to escalate. It would eventually explode.

In the second game of the season, we were playing the Jets in Three Rivers when a pass bounced off me and into the hands of a defensive back named Michael Brim, who took the ball seventy-seven yards to the house.

We still won the game by seventeen, but Erhardt could not let go of my mistake. He came up to me during stretches the following Wednesday and pointed to Bill Cowher on the other side of the field.

"You're lucky that guy is your head coach," he said. "If it was Bill Parcells, you'd be gone for that crap you pulled Sunday."

"Really?" I said, and then pointed to Barry Foster, whom Ron loved. "Then what would he do with your boy Barry?"

Barry had fumbled three times in the game.

Erhardt walked away silently. But he wasn't done.

We were playing the Chargers in San Diego the following Sunday and they had a smart, hard-hitting safety named Stanley "the Sheriff" Richard. One of the job hazards of running the ball is being held up while defenders take free shots on exposed and defenseless parts of your body. The safety is often the dealer of such blows. In the first half of the game, Richard followed suit. I carried the ball twice and he lit me up both times after other defenders had tied me up.

I hadn't forgotten the hits when we rolled into the second half. On a third down and long, Neil O'Donnell threw me the ball on a flare route to our side of the field. As I turned up the sideline I saw Richard coming at me with a full head of steam. With one move I could have avoided him and made the first down. I didn't care about the first down.

I veered right into Richard and hit him so hard, I knocked him out of the game.

Erhardt went nuts. He started screaming names at me and berating me for not making the first down.

I jumped up and threw the ball down.

"Screw your first down!" I screamed back. "He's been teeing off on me all day."

I got in Ron's face with some choice words until Cowher came over and broke it up.

"He's been on my case since he got here," I asserted to Cowher. "I'm done with it!"

"Just calm down and let's win this game," Bill replied. "We'll deal with this later."

Cowher was a man of his word, and on Tuesday he called me

into his office and let me air everything out. He then told me he had already talked to Ron and instructed him to keep his mouth shut where I was concerned. He also explained that the coaches had watched the film and everyone, including Ron, understood why I did what I did to the Chargers' safety. Bill concluded our meeting assuring me I would be a Steeler as long as he was the coach. Even though this would not hold true, it was through no fault of his.

I was glad to get everything out in the open, but in truth the only thing that changed was that Erhardt no longer vocalized his displeasure with me. He found other ways to convey it throughout that year and into the following year—until our twelfth game of the season against his former boss's New England Patriots.

Barry Foster was again out with an injury, and Leroy Thompson and I had taken over the running load during game eight. My biggest game of the 1993 season was four games later against the Patriots. I scored twice and tallied 100 yards of total offense. After the game Parcells walked across the field to shake Ron's hand.

"Hoge is one heck of a football player," Parcells insisted. "You don't win this game if not for him."

Erhardt changed his ways after that game and began to talk to me about Barry and me being a two-back tandem the following year. It was a plan that never came to fruition. The real reasons underscored the growing divide between the old and new NFL.

Walter Payton was paid $1 million in 1987, the last year of his contract and my first year in the league. He was one of only seven million-dollar players in the NFL that year.[2] When I became a free agent after the 1993 season, his Chicago Bears offered me $3.1 million for a three-year contract. While the advent of unrestricted free agency and collective bargaining had skyrocketed players' salaries in the six years since Payton's retirement, I was still flattered by the Bears' offer because I was no Sweetness.

My dilemma was that I wanted to stay with the Steelers.

They wanted to keep me but had only offered me $1.5 million for three years with $100K to sign. It was significantly less than I had made the previous three years and half of what the Bears had offered.

I went to Tom Donahoe, the Steelers' director of football operations, and told him I would take less money than the Bears offered to stay with the Steelers—$2.5 million for three years, along with a smaller signing bonus. He looked at me like a second-class citizen.

"You're not gonna get that Chicago deal," he retorted. "Besides, I have Barry Foster now. Why do I need you?"

I immediately turned and marched out of the Steelers' front office. As soon as my foot hit the parking lot, I dialed my agent.

He answered and I announced, "I'm a Bear," then hung up.

To understand my reaction, you should know that Barry Foster had walked out on our team the previous season. After spraining his ankle in the eighth game—the third sidelining injury of his three-and-a-half-year-old career—he announced he was done playing for the season. He then packed his bags and drove home to Dallas. His decision to walk out was not overlooked by his teammates—especially those of us who'd been around when guys like Walter Payton, Mike Webster, and Donnie Shell still played.

It was appropriate I would spend my final season with the Chicago Bears, as it seemed I was fighting to represent a dying breed of player so precisely embodied in the greatest running back of all time and Chicago's finest son.

When you hold up a back like Barry Foster against the backdrop of Walter Payton, the contrast is so stark it seems they never played the same game. This is partly true. By the time I was headed to the Bears, the NFL had become not only a players' game, it was becoming a media juggernaut with a new multibillion-dollar television contract with the Fox network.

Dying were the days when players held mantras like Payton's "Never die easy." It seemed "Get rich quick" was becoming common, and with the new perspective came a change in the passion and will of players coming into the league. To a growing number, professional football had become a lottery ticket that just needed rubbing for a couple years. Get into the league, get paid, and get out.

Playing the game well was never about money for me.

I will admit that after Donahoe's smug reply, I wanted to beat down the entire Steelers organization. I'd have felt justified in that moment. Fortunately, I took a step back before doing anything self-serving and stupid.

I vowed I would never play the prima donna role, as if somebody owed me something. The fact was that Tom Donahoe, not the Steelers, was choosing not to re-sign me. Not the Rooneys. Not Chuck Noll or Dick Hoak or Bill Cowher. I wasn't going to punish the greatest organization in football over one man's opinion.

The Steelers had taken a chance on me, a "too small and too slow" farm boy from Idaho. They handed me the keys to my dreams and I would always be grateful for that, even if I would not finish my career with them.

The day after I signed with the Bears was like a thumbs-up from God. I was in the locker room packing my things when Dan Rooney called me into his office.

"Merril," he said, "I wish we could have done things differently. I wish we had never let you go. If you need anything, these doors are always open to you."

His words meant the world to me and they confirmed my decision to honor the organization and people that had given me so much. They had become family, and while families don't always remain in the same town, they remain bonded by mutual respect, mutual trust, and mutual gratitude.

This is something so many in today's NFL have forgotten. Back then, they were just beginning to forget.

But a few of us kept remembering.

The growing gap was never more evident in my career than in the Bears' training camp the following year.

More Than Smarts and Skill

T he backs were running a conditioning drill to simulate game experience: explode for forty yards as fast as we could, then recover for thirty-five seconds, then repeat. Sweat was pouring and our legs were burning. It was the second practice of the day in the fifth week of training camp, and hundreds of fans framed the practice fields to preview the 1994 team. We were halfway through our drill when Coach Joe Pendry, the backs coach for the Bears, stopped us and called out to a rookie running back.

"Robbie, how old are you?"

"Twenty-two, Coach," the rookie replied.

"And how fast do you run the forty?"

"Four-point-two, Coach!" The kid announced. He had every reason to be proud—only a handful of players in NFL history have that kind of blazing speed.

Coach Pendry then turned to me.

"Merril, how fast do you run the forty?"

Here we go, I thought to myself. *He's putting the writing on the wall: old guy out, new guy in. I'm not playing this game.*

I didn't answer.

"C'mon, Hoge," Pendry prodded. "Okay, how many games have you played in the NFL?"

"One hundred and eight," I said.

"How many practices have you missed?"

"I haven't missed one since my freshman year in college."

"And remind me," he continued, "how old are you?"

"I'll be thirty in January." I wasn't sure where he was going.

"You're almost thirty? Really?" He spoke in a high voice for effect. "Okay then, what was your fastest forty time *ever*?"

"Four-point-five-eight," I said. It was my time during a private workout for the Packers before the 1987 draft.

Coach Pendry then proceeded to bring his demonstration to the attention of everyone watching.

In a loud voice he announced, "The fastest Hoge has ever run is a 4.58, and the rookie runs a 4.2."

He then paused and deadpanned at the rookie: "Robbie, can you explain something to me? If you run a 4.2 and the fastest Hoge has ever run is 4.58, why is it that he beats you every time we run this drill?"

The rookie stood silent while Pendry brought his point home.

"I'm asking because when we cut you next week, I want to make sure you know why."

I immediately flashed back to watching an interview with Walter Payton when I was a teenager. He'd been asked what made him better than the rest. I'd never forgotten his response.

"It's really simple," he replied. "I want it more than they do on Monday, Tuesday, Wednesday, Thursday, Friday, and Saturday. You just see Sunday."

I then remembered the one time I met Walter Payton. I was a rookie with the Steelers, and we'd just been slaughtered in a preseason game at Soldier Field. I ran up to him at midfield after the game. I shook his hand and started talking his head off. I told him I idolized him growing up...had a Bears lamp by my bedside as a boy...ran dirt hills the way he did...watched tapes of him. There was an awkward silence when I finished. Then he spoke in that soft voice of his.

"That is the nicest thing anyone has ever said to me, Merril. Thank you for taking the time to come over here and tell me that."

I didn't know how to end the conversation, so I asked for an autograph.

"Well," he replied, "I don't have a pen on me right now—but I'd like to give you these." He slid off his wristbands and elbow pads and handed them to me.

We'd just lost 50–0 and I went bounding back to the locker room like I'd just won the Super Bowl.

Walter was the one player I hoped to emulate more than any other. He epitomized the untainted passion of an old schooler.

Standing there on that Bears practice field in 1994—eight seasons later—it suddenly hit me that Coach Pendry's demonstration had ascribed a similar message to my career. It validated all I had given to play the game I loved. It also explained why the rookie never accomplished anything worth remembering.

There eventually comes an obstacle for which outstanding skill and intellect are not enough unless they are channeled through a passion-fueled will. Payton summed it up with his motto, "Never die easy." Mine was "Find a way." The words are different but they underscore the same reality: great will is worth more than smarts and skill.

I would soon have to apply the truth in a context I never imagined.

Staggered and blinking, I didn't know what hit me. I'd caught a pass in the second quarter and turned upfield. Two defenders flashed toward me and I put my head down to run through them. Now I was flat on my back, staring up at my teammate Tim Worley. He took one look at me and waved over the Bears' medical staff.

The ground was shaking beneath me like a massive earth-quake. I gripped the earth but could not find my balance. Buoy-ancy, however, was automatic. With all the mental focus I could muster, I pushed my wobbling body upright and joined the huddle before the ref could call an injury time-out. I staggered through two more plays. The field goal team then came onto the field.

What happened next was told to me weeks later. To this day, I remember nothing.

I walked to the sidelines and told our trainers I'd been hit in the head.

They walked me to the bench and started quizzing me.

"Merril," one of them said, "do you know where you are?"

"Yeah," I said, "Florida."

"How do you know?"

"Because I can hear the ocean."

The trainers immediately escorted me to the locker room. It was the third game of the preseason and we were playing in Kansas City.

As I sat in the locker room my teammates came in to go over halftime adjustments. I observed them as if I was behind glass. I didn't move. Didn't talk. Didn't interact. Then the team doctors approached and started asking me questions. The same questions over and over. I had only the realization that I was being asked the same thing. I could not, however, remember my previous answers. Some questions I could not answer at all.

The trainers asked me to dress and they escorted me to the hospital, where I had a brain scan. I don't remember traveling to the hospital, but once there I had a constant nervous feeling, like when you're worried someone is about to find you out. Everyone from the trainers to the staff doctors to the triage nurse was bombarding me with the same questions I had been asked before. I started to get paranoid. I was stuck in Groundhog Day.

How did I feel?

What was my name?

Where was I?

Did I know what had happened?

I felt like a moron. I didn't know the answers but I knew enough to know I should.

After the checkup and scans, a nurse handed me a manila envelope and asked me to take a seat in the waiting room.

I was surprised when a moment later a Bears team doctor came running by the waiting room door. He spotted me and stopped on a dime.

"There you are!" he exclaimed, out of breath. "We've been looking for you—do you have your scans?"

Finally, I was confident of an answer. I reached to my side to grab them.

They weren't there. I felt on the other side of my seat. Nothing. I looked up in disbelief. I felt as if I had been shocked with a stun gun.

The doctor explained I had wandered and gone missing. I was sitting in another waiting room three floors above where the nurse first left me. He and others had been frantically looking for me. My scans were sitting next to my seat in the original waiting room.

The football game was over now, he said, and the team plane was loaded and waiting to leave.

Despite headaches and flulike symptoms during the subsequent days, I was back in practice a week later. I never saw a neurologist. I never had another scan.

My prognosis was determined on a phone call with the Bears

team doctor five days after the hit. He asked me how I felt. I told him I felt fine. I was cleared to play.

I was utterly naïve about the danger of what I was doing. I knew only one way to play, and pain had never stood in the way. It still wouldn't—even though I would soon learn this was a different kind of pain.

I got myself ready to play the first regular season game thirteen days later and keep my streak of consecutive games intact—the longest current streak in the NFL at that time. I then gritted out the first three regular-season games, numbers 109, 110, and 111 of my career.

I pushed myself to perform, but outside my specific role in each play, I could not hold information in my head. At that point in my career, I had become the type of player who knew what everyone was doing on every play. Now suddenly the snap count was difficult to remember. Thinking beyond the direction I should run or the linebacker I should block was like piling marbles on a wet paper napkin in my mind. I had no idea this was information I should have been sharing with the medical staff. I felt as if I would lose all my marbles any second.

Eventually I did. But before that happened, I continued pushing through the bumps, bruises, and one more break.

I rubbed a blister on my foot over the next week, and every day the medical staff looked at that blister. They cleaned it, put bandages on it, and retaped it. It was a daily concern. Another concern arose as well.

We were playing the Jets in the Meadowlands in the fourth game of the regular season when I caught a pass out of the backfield and turned up the Jets sideline. A defender shoved me out of bounds right at one of his teammates standing on the sideline. I realized at the last second the guy wasn't going to move an inch. I stuck out my left hand to brace myself and he threw his shoulder into me. I felt a sudden sting in the palm of my hand.

Once I came back under control, I squeezed my left hand into a fist to test the pain. Not bad. I jogged onto the field and tossed the ball to the ref before joining the huddle.

As our quarterback relayed the next play, I reached down to pull up my left thigh pad. There was a sharp sting. It felt like the middle of my hand separated from my fingers. I knew I'd broken my hand. I played out the series, then went to the sideline and told the trainer my hand was broken and I'd need them to look at it at halftime. It was halfway through the second quarter.

In the locker room at halftime, I walked back to the training room and they took X-rays. A trainer came out after talking with the doctor.

"Your hand is broken!" he exclaimed. The bone to my ring finger was broken in the middle of my palm.

"I know," I said. "I told you guys that on the field."

"I thought you were kidding," he replied. "You can't play with this."

"I just finished playing half a quarter with it," I replied. "I can finish the game."

"But you run the risk of the bone settling into your hand and your knuckle disappearing."

"Would that be a big deal?" I asked.

"No," he said after a pause. "It would just look a little odd."

I was willing to take that chance, so I went back out after halftime and finished the game. We beat the Jets 19–7. As the team was showering and dressing, I had my hand wrapped in ice while the doctor and trainers discussed casting my hand the next morning.

"No way am I letting you cast my hand," I asserted.

The thought of having any part of my body imprisoned had always been too much for me. In fact, it was one of the primary reasons I trained and played so hard. I always felt that if I was in the best shape possible and played at a hundred miles per hour, my chances of being hurt greatly diminished. The only injury I ever truly worried about was blowing out a knee. So I also always made sure I was in the best football position when hitting with someone—knees bent and hips low so that my knee joints were always in the strongest position. I believed if I played in top shape and perfect position at maximum effort, I could last a long time in the league. A little broken bone wasn't going to keep me from playing with my full faculties.

The team medical staff and I brainstormed until we came to a solution. We would design a cast that would protect the middle of my hand but still allow me to catch and carry the ball.

I went home, and that night it came to me that if we slid a U-shaped cast sideways across my hand, the broken bone in my palm would be protected and my fingers would retain freedom to grip the ball. The following morning, the medical staff fashioned the makeshift cast and taped it on. We tested it out in practice and I never missed a beat.

Throughout my football career, I felt that as long as I knew the risks associated with an injury, and the danger of playing with it was limited to pain, it was a minor risk. While a broken hand on a quarterback would typically be a sidelining injury, to me it was an injury I could mitigate and a pain I could push through.

However, I was about to learn the hard way there is one kind of injury that cannot be mitigated with makeshift casts or mind over matter. It is a serious sidelining injury regardless of a player's poise or position.

When asked what the most vital organ in the body is, most would say the heart. Most would be wrong. The most vital organ in your body is the brain. Yet most teams in the NFL have historically treated it no better than a blister or a hand bone.

A spinal injury is considered the most serious injury in football. We have seen the immediate and tangible effects of this: paralysis. It's hard to forget a player who goes limp and can no longer move his limbs.

Brain injury is different. Its worst effects are often delayed, sometimes for years. We rarely see a disabled, incapacitated player after a concussion, so "out of sight, out of mind" often follows suit. In fact, if a player is knocked out on the field but regains consciousness, he usually walks off the field on his own. He'll be fine, we say. At worst, we've only seen him dizzy and a little disoriented, like a cartoon character seeing stars after taking a hammer to the head. After the game he fields questions at a press conference. He jokes. He smiles. All appears well. The problem is that all is not always well on the inside.

It seems neither the football world nor the medical profession began considering this fact until the great "Iron" Mike Webster died in 2002. Even then it was not a startling wake-up call.

At the time of his retirement in 1990, Iron Mike was already showing signs of the brain damage noted in his medical files before his career ended. After his retirement, his mental and psychological health declined rapidly. He suffered from amnesia, dementia, throbbing headaches, hearing loss, and depression. At times, wrote ESPN.com's Greg Garber, he became so desperate for a reprieve that he "repeatedly stunned himself, sometimes a dozen times, into unconsciousness with a black Taser gun."[1]

The sad and unfortunate conclusion to Iron Mike's life has been well documented. He lost his marriage, his money, his businesses, and even his dignity, sleeping in a train station and his pickup truck off and on over an eighteen-month span.

In an interview during the final years of his life, his son Garrett recalled frustration when Webster missed his tenth birthday party just three years after his retirement. "He didn't even call me and I was mad," he admitted. "Now I understand that there was something wrong." Instead of enjoying cake and ice cream with his growing boy, Webster was lying half-conscious on a Budgetel Inn bed with a prescription drug cocktail in his system and a bucket of vomit by his side.[2]

Doctors have estimated that over his twenty-five-year football career at the high school, college, and professional levels,

Webster's brain sustained the equivalent of 25,000 car accidents.[3] And we're now learning Webster was not the only one.

In January 2009, former Tampa Bay Buccaneers offensive lineman Tom McHale was found to have suffered from what is called chronic traumatic encephalopathy (CTE) in the years leading up to his early death. While he died at forty-five from what police called an accidental overdose, his self-medicating began when he started feeling the effects of the repetitive head traumas he suffered during his football career, nine years of which he spent in the NFL.

Dr. Ann C. McKee, a codirector of the Boston University medical group that conducted the postmortem pathology, indicated a probable link between McHale's brain damage and his self-destructive habits in the final years of his life. "You would expect," she said of the damage her team found, "the symptoms of lack of insight, poor judgment, decreased concentration and attention, inability to multitask and memory problems."[4]

All told, six former NFL players who died in recent years have been found to have suffered from CTE—also known as "punch-drunk syndrome"—either during or shortly after their playing days. Along with Mike Webster and Tom McHale, the brains of former Oilers linebacker John Grimsley, former Eagles defensive back Andre Waters, and former Steelers offensive linemen Terry Long and Justin Strzelczyk each showed pronounced CTE. In each case the player's on-the-field victories were sadly overshadowed by tragic and untimely deaths related to brain damage they sustained while playing the game they loved.

Webster went silently and sadly alone at fifty, a shell of his former self, unable to fend off the demons of his chronic pain and mental deterioration. McHale took his own life at forty-five while trying to preserve it. Grimsley, also forty-five, accidentally shot himself in the chest while cleaning his gun, an accident his wife is convinced was related to his increasing memory loss in the months prior.[5] Waters shot himself in the head at forty-four. An autopsy showed his brain tissue had degenerated into that of an eighty-five-year old man.[6] Long committed suicide at forty-five by drinking antifreeze. Strzelczyk swerved his car into an oncoming tanker at ninety miles per hour while trying to evade police. Toxicology reports showed his erratic behavior was not the result of drugs or alcohol.[7]

Clearly the effects of concussions should be taken no less seriously than neck injuries. Both the NFL and the medical profession have made educational strides since these men played. More is being done to help players avoid similar fates. In 1994, however, head traumas were still treated with less attention than a tiny bone in my hand. I suffered the consequences.

Five weeks after my Kansas City concussion, I would traumatize my head again, this time at home on Soldier Field in the fifth game of the season. While I had returned from the vicious hit by the late, great Derrick Thomas, the perilous effects still lingered like plaque in an artery. I was on borrowed time and didn't know it, and the doctors hadn't told me. I was about to play the last game of my NFL career—and nearly my life.

Leading up to our fifth game, we installed a running play to take advantage of a weakness we saw in the Buffalo Bills' defense. The play was out of the I-formation, and I would be the lead blocker for Lewis Tillman, the tailback. At the snap, we would start right to get the defense moving one way and then bend it back to the left. Based on films, we expected the safety to be the only remaining defender on the left perimeter, putting us in a two-on-one advantage. We perfected the play in practice, and when it came time to run it in the game, we were confident of a good gain. Plays always work in practice. Games are another story.

On October 2, 1994, the ball was snapped and everything fell into place as we predicted it would—until Tillman and I reached the left-side perimeter.

The safety was there as we expected, but he was stacked directly behind the cornerback, who had come off his coverage to help. The two-on-one advantage was gone. Still, momentum was in our favor. We had a full head of steam, and they were waiting for us to make a move. In an instant I decided that if I drove through the legs of the cornerback, I could take him and the safety out with one block. I lowered my body and ran as hard as I could at the corner's thigh pads.

It is the last thing I remember on the field.

Somehow I rejoined the huddle, ran another play, and then came to the sideline where the trainers discovered my face mask was mangled. It looked as if someone had taken a sledgehammer to it. The trainers sat me down and began to remove the mask and affix a replacement. That's when they noticed a large gash in my chin that was pouring blood.

As they worked quickly to get my helmet and face patched up for our next offensive series, the trainers started talking to me about the game and asking me questions about my chin. I didn't respond. They asked again, thinking I must have been daydreaming. Again, no response. I stared into the stands. They ushered me straight to the locker room.

A teammate who'd hurt his ankle earlier in the game was already there. The trainers sat me on the edge of the training table opposite him. I remember glancing over.

"Hey man," he said with concern in his voice, "you feeling all right?"

I heard the question but couldn't formulate an answer. *I'm not going to make it,* I thought to myself.

Then my eyes started to flutter and I lost consciousness.

I dropped from the table to the locker room floor and stopped breathing.

I had no pulse. The trainer went to apply CPR when I started breathing again.

I sat up and then stood with their help. The trainers walked me straight to the ambulance.

I spent the rest of the day and night in intensive care while the hospital staff monitored my vitals. I could not identify anyone I loved: not my brother Marty, my daughter, Kori, or my wife, Toni.

The hospital released me two days later under the supervision of the Bears' team doctors. They scheduled a visit to a neurologist in Chicago. After reviewing my case, the neurologist told me I could take the season off and return the next year. At that point, however, I trusted neither the Bears' medical staff nor any of their referrals.

I wasn't fully aware of what had happened to me, but I knew

something was seriously wrong. I could not keep simple thoughts in my head, couldn't remember what I had done a minute before, and still had difficulty recalling names of everyday items and people I had known all my life. I couldn't name the president of the United States.

At my request, the Bears' doctors made an appointment for the following week with Dr. Joseph Maroon, the longtime Steelers team physician and the chairman of neurosurgery at Allegheny General Hospital in Pittsburgh. He immediately referred me to his colleague Dr. Mark Lovell, a neuropsychologist at the same hospital who, along with Dr. Maroon, had created a cognitive test that measured brain functionality after major head trauma.

The Steelers were the first NFL team to administer such a test on their players. When Bubby Brister suffered a concussion in 1990, Dr. Maroon told Coach Noll he could not clear Bubby to play the following week against the Dallas Cowboys. In an interview with the *Pittsburgh Post-Gazette*'s Jack Kelly, Dr. Maroon recalls Noll's response:

> Noll asked me, "Why can't he?"
> I said, "Well, the guidelines say such and such...."
> He said, "Who wrote the guidelines?"
> And then he basically said, "Look, Maroon. If you want me to keep an athlete out of football, I want objective data that you can show me indicating that there is something wrong with his cognitive abilities."[8]

Dr. Maroon consulted Dr. Lovell, and the two found that there was no such objective cognitive test. So the two set out to create one, and Noll agreed to have all the Steelers players take it to establish a baseline. The test has been updated several times since 1990 and now is known as the ImPACT (Immediate Post-concussion Assessment and Cognitive Testing), the only mandatory cognitive test required of all NHL and NFL athletes. Back then the test offered the only legitimate measurement of the real effects of a concussion.

Because I was on that 1990 Steelers team required to take Drs. Maroon and Lovell's original test, the doctors had a baseline measurement of my cognitive abilities. In other words, they knew how my brain worked when nothing was wrong.

When Dr. Lovell retested me in 1994, after my second concussion in five weeks, the results were sobering. In 1990, I scored in the 90–100 percent proficiency range on every question—the highest of any Steelers player. When I retook the test after the second head trauma, my scores all fell between 40 and 50 percent.

Dr. Lovell looked at me somberly. "I have seen people thrown through windshields with less brain damage."

I met with Dr. Maroon shortly thereafter.

"Merril," he said, "I could not lay my head down at night if I let you on that field again. I can't let you play anymore. It's over."

He didn't even want to discuss what might happen if I suffered another concussion.

From that point on, I had a different sort of pain to fight through: the releasing of a lifelong dream.

What might give greatest testimony to how affected I was by the head trauma, now nearly two weeks after the Bills game, was my grossly uncharacteristic emotions during those days. Case in point, when Dr. Maroon told me it was over, the first emotion I felt was apathy. I simply accepted his words as though he had merely told me I had to have an X-ray. "It's over," he said, and I sat there thinking, *Oh well*. My actual response to Dr. Maroon was simply "Okay."

The strangest part is that I could hear myself accepting the sentence and a voice inside me was screaming, *Are you kidding me? That is your reaction? You've just been told you will never play the game you love again! You have sacrificed so much and worked so hard for so long, and all you're going to say is "Okay"?*

The debate waged on inside me over the next two weeks, but I was helpless to do or say anything about it.

On Monday, October 17, 1994, I flew back to Chicago to meet with Coach Dave Wannstedt and Bears president Michael McCaskey. We agreed it was best to announce my retirement immediately and place me on Injured Reserve. I felt as if I had been drugged. These decisions were being made about ending my lifelong dream and I could not stop them. I was apathetic and numb, going along with whatever people suggested I do. I met with the team shortly thereafter. I managed to remain lucid for a brief period and share my heart with my football family.

I didn't want to give them a rah-rah speech and tell them to go out and play for me. First and foremost, I wanted them to know that I would do whatever I could for them. They were still my teammates, and while I would no longer be donning a jersey and standing alongside them on the field, I would support and promote them in any way I could.

Second, I wanted them to recognize that when you're in the

midst of the season, you often forget things can be taken away so quickly. I reminded them they were 4-2, and at 4-2 they had a great chance to win the division and go on to win a championship. "Seize that opportunity now," I insisted. "Don't think past this year. Give your all now. And do it for yourselves and for each other."

After I gave the news to my teammates, the Bears held a press conference in which I made my retirement public. Months later, I saw pictures and watched clips of me in front of Halas Hall addressing the media. I read articles filled with the things I said. It was a strange, violating feeling, like observing somebody who had hijacked my body.

To this day, I don't remember a single detail of the press conference. Maybe my lack of cognitive presence during that time was a blessing in disguise. Maybe it was God's way of nudging me down a path I would have likely tried to fight with everything in me, perhaps to my own grave harm.

It would be bad enough as it was. Looking back, I cannot imagine worse.

While the immediate proceedings of my retirement were a sudden and strange out-of-body experience, I was fully aware of one thing. I did not have any regrets about my football career. That the game was over for me was tough to grasp, but the untimely nature of my departure came without remorse.

I knew then what I know now. I made the absolute most of my talents and opportunities. And I played hard on every down I ever played. I once read that Coach Wannstedt affirmed this at my retirement press conference when he told the media that I was always the first to arrive at Halas Hall at six a.m. and one of the last to leave. It was this way for me throughout my career. I left nothing to chance and found a way to be my best from the beginning to the unexpected end. The fact that I can still say this today is invaluable to me.

Yet, despite the comfort this brought me during the post-NFL transition, and despite the pseudocomfort of my emotional numbness, I would soon come to see that what stood before me was perhaps more daunting than any challenge I had ever faced. The life I had dreamed about since I was a small boy was over—and I was not yet thirty years old.

As my emotional faculties slowly returned in the weeks following my retirement, letting go of the game I loved, the game I'd played since I was eight years old, became an enormous challenge. I hadn't planned on the timing. It was midfall. I was in full-scale football mode. For nearly two decades, I had known no other mode during this season. What mode fit now? What was the next step on a path I hadn't planned on traveling yet?

I was again being reminded that circumstances don't make or break you; they reveal you. As I slowly healed, I would learn that rising to some challenges requires the combination of every lesson you've learned, every resource you own, and strong faith.

Before my career ended, I would have said that getting to the NFL was my greatest victory. I had overcome many challenges before becoming a Steeler—my father's absence...the near loss of my hand...my mother's death...playing for an unknown college program with a less-than-ideal NFL skill set. I believed winning those battles prepared me to realize my dream of playing professional football.

I was shortsighted.

While my time in the NFL was a dream come true, it was not the culmination of a lifetime of desires. I was only twenty-nine at the time of my retirement. Life was not even half over.

The game gave me privileges I never imagined, but it was ultimately one large mountain along a longer and higher path. There would be other mountains to climb, some larger than I had ever known. My preparation for them was the twenty-nine-year path I had traveled thus far—which included more than seven successful seasons in the NFL.

During this time I recalled a story I was told just days before my career-ending concussion. Thinking back now, perhaps it was a prophetic metaphor about me, with an ending I would need to write for myself.

One of the things I loved about my brief stint playing for the Bears was having the head trainer, Fred Caito, tell me Walter Payton stories while he was taping me before practice. One morning, I hopped on the training table and said, "Okay, Fred, fire away."

A teammate named Maurice "Mo" Douglas then piped in.

"I got one for you," he said. And he told this story: "I was just like you," he began. "I loved Payton and wanted to be just like him. So when the Bears drafted me, I wanted to meet him right away and when I did, the first thing I asked is if I could train with him.

"Walter said, 'Sure,' so we set a date and a time and I showed up early, I was so excited. Payton then pulled up in his red Ferrari and stepped out wearing his Roos sweatband with matching sweats and wristbands. He looked sweet. The first thing we did was warm up, and then we walked over to the famous hill he trained on. He explained the goal was to run up the hill as fast as you could and then rest on your walk back down. So we exploded up the hill. My heart was beating out of my chest as we reached the top. I could barely breathe. I looked over at Payton and he was breathing with ease, like he'd never taken a step.

"On the way back down I caught my breath and asked him how many we were going to do. Payton looked over and said, 'Ten.'

"As soon as we reached the bottom, we turned around and headed back up. I got halfway up the hill and turned around, walked back down, puked, and then got in my car and went home."

When Mo finished telling the story he said something I never forgot.

"The difference between Walter and me," he confessed, "was that he wanted it more than me."

Now I was suddenly out of the league but, strangely, I stood before a similar daunting hill. The questions would ultimately boil down to how bad I wanted to climb it.

The head trauma that ended my career reverberated for months. Doctors said it left me in the mental state of a seven-year old. I spent six months reading to my three-year old daughter every night to become literate again. I spent weeks relearning names, faces, and phone numbers I'd known all my life. I couldn't even remember how to use a checkbook. If I drove anywhere— even to the most routine locations near my home—I would get disoriented. The circumstances eventually got to me.

I lay on the couch day in and day out, empty-headed and purposeless. I wouldn't work out. I wouldn't change clothes. I ate very little. I wasn't suicidal, but I lost all passion for life. It was a dark time and I felt incapable of doing anything about it.

What I would soon learn was that I was suffering from clinical depression brought on by what I believe was a combination of postconcussion syndrome and a sudden loss of purpose.

I went from waking up in the dark of the morning and trying to accomplish more than those studs in the Army do by eight a.m. to lying around with zero drive to do anything.

I can honestly say I have never been out of shape. Personal health and fitness have been and always will be a passion of mine, but for weeks I let myself go and did nothing but watch *Barney* with Kori for hours at a time.

It took a familiar voice and a speech I'd heard dozens of times to wake me up again.

8

Finding Your Life's Work

C oach Noll pressed the lesson into our minds above all else. He'd give the speech in the first days of training camp or after a big loss or at the conclusion of the season when players would go their separate ways. "Find your life's work, men," he'd say, "because no matter how long you play this game, the majority of your life will be spent doing something other than playing football."

I didn't understand the magnitude of his words until the fall of 1994. After nearly two months of numb emotions and stale behavior, I was struck with the realization that no one was calling to offer me the next chapter of my life.

There was nothing magical about the moment. I believe I simply began to attach tangible feelings to my circumstances again. My deepest emotions began to rise to the surface and finally regain their voice.

Taking action had been something that was never difficult

for me. Not when I was eight years old and not when a bone snapped in my hand in my final season in the NFL. Then, for two months, it was nearly impossible.

Now it was utterly necessary. I was veering off the bending road before me and I knew the first step was taking some sort of action. The question was: what action?

I thought back on Noll's speeches on a life's work. It was as if I were there again in the Steelers' team meeting room at the end of another season. "Most of you will spend the majority of your lives doing something other than football."

I was now entering that majority. What was my "something"? This was certainly not the first time I had considered it. From the moment I first heard those words as a green rookie in the League, my life's work was a constant in my mind.

Earlier in my NFL career, I thought I might find it in insurance. If it was good enough for my father, I thought to myself, it should be good enough for me. After my second season with the Steelers, I set up a meeting with an insurance agent near my off-season home in Pittsburgh.

I walked into the meeting with a firm handshake and good intentions. My best friend, Jeff Spadafore, came at my request to help me formulate an unemotional, educated decision about this industry into which I might invest my off-seasons and potentially my life after the NFL.

After exchanging five minutes of small talk, the agent reached beneath his desk and retrieved a ten-inch-thick binder full of rules, regulations, and numerical tabs. He slapped it on the desk in front of me along with six books.

"If you're going to work in insurance," he asserted, "you will need to familiarize yourself with this."

I glanced over at my buddy in the seat next to me. My suddenly frozen countenance said it all. He knew precisely what I was thinking. There was no way on earth I was going to read even one inch of that binder, let alone the other nine.

I kindly thanked the man for his time and we left the building. It had become crystal clear to me that my future would in no way entail selling insurance.

Fortunately, insurance was not the only path I tested.

One path in particular came to the forefront.

When I was a rookie, I agreed to sign autographs on the showroom of a local car dealership and WBZZ (B94), a Pittsburgh radio station, was doing a remote broadcast there as well. The host of B94's evening drive time asked me if I would like to call in on Fridays and talk about the upcoming game. The show didn't conflict with any team obligations, so I said sure. Every Friday that season, I would call in and talk about who we were playing, how we were preparing, and some general thoughts about the significance of the game itself. I was one of the first Steelers to do this on a weekly basis, and we learned the fans liked hearing a player talk about the game. The show became very popular.

The summer after my rookie season, I was doing another autograph signing for the local car dealership, and this time WDVE, Pittsburgh's famous rock station, was also there. A representative of the station came up to me and asked how much B94 paid me to come on their show each week.

B94 paid me nothing—but I'm dumb, not stupid, so under my breath, with the confidence of a mouse, I muttered, "Ten thousand."

The rep perked up. "Would you be willing to do our morning show for fifteen thousand?"

He quickly had himself a deal.

The agreement had one stipulation. I was required to come into the station on Monday before practice. When I first heard this, I was not particularly looking forward to getting up even earlier than I already did. But the station was on the way to the stadium and I was, after all, being paid for the gig. I got myself up at five a.m. that first Monday and made my way there. The drive would soon become no problem at all.

I walked into that studio for the first time and something came over me. I observed the guys at the board behind the glass. I watched Jim Krenn and Scott Paulsen at the mikes with their headsets on. They were laughing and enjoying themselves. I knew this was something I wanted to do when I was through playing football.

Six autumns after my first trip to the WDVE studio, I stood from my couch and walked downstairs to my office. I sat in front of my computer and began piecing together my first professional résumé. By this time I had expanded my postfootball career options to three: coaching, fitness training, and broadcasting. I told myself that if opportunities arose in broadcasting, coaching and fitness training would have to wait.

I contacted everyone I could think of in these three fields.

I had little success early on, but the mere act accelerated the emotional healing process. Contrary to what we think, it is often easier to act your way into feeling than to feel your way into acting. If I had waited until I felt like taking the next step down the unknown path before me, my life would not look the same today. In fact, like some of my fellow athletes who had suffered similar head traumas during their playing days, I might not have ever recovered.

It is an eerie thought that three of the six former NFL players who suffered from pronounced CTE before their tragic deaths were men I knew well. All three were offensive linemen with the Steelers. Iron Mike Webster was my preseason road-game roommate when I was a rookie. Terry Long set me up on my first date as a Steeler. Justin Strzelczyk and I became fast friends when he joined the Steelers three years after me.

I stood across the huddle from all three men dozens of times. I can still see their eyes behind their masks. They were fierce warriors on the field of play who I know heard Noll's same "life's work" speech many times.

To this day, I am not sure why these three men were not able to recover from their concussion-induced depression and I was. I only know that taking the simple steps of faith to send out my résumé and make some humbling phone calls was part of it. Things eventually began to happen, and while progress was an intense and frustrating struggle, the fight reignited my passion for life and reminded me of my responsibilities and capabilities.

Yes, I was depressed. I was hurting emotionally and

physically. I could not think straight. I could barely read two sentences in a children's book. I did not know what lay ahead.

I would make no excuses.

I would go forward anyway, with the skill, intellect, and will I had acquired in my twenty-nine years. I would control what I could. As for the rest, I would have faith. What I did not know and could not see were in God's hands.

A stark reminder of this came a few days after I sent out my résumé. I was attending a charity wine-tasting event I had committed to earlier in the season. I don't drink, but I knew getting out of the house would be good for me. While I was there, one of the wine pourers talked me into trying one of the high-dollar wines. He filled the bottom of a glass and handed it to me. I lifted it to my mouth. As soon as the smell of the fermented grapes hit my nasal cavity, I went blind.

I grabbed for the table in front of me and set down the glass. Fear shot through my body. I started rubbing my eyes and blinking intermittently, trying to make myself see when I knew my eyes were open. I saw only blackness.

Finally, after an eternal half minute, my sight returned. Clearly, there was more going on than I knew. I had a long road of recovery ahead.

I also had a choice: shrink back in fear of the unknown or put one foot in front of the other.

I kept walking. The unknown had never stopped me before. It would not now.

In December, roughly six weeks after sending out my résumé, I got a call from my agent. Fox wanted me to do color for the Seahawks-Bucs game with Mike Bream. Although I knew little about broadcasting for live games, I flew to Seattle a few days later, thrilled at the opportunity.

It was a good scenario to start. I had played against every one of the players on the field. Some had even been teammates of mine. But the scenario didn't play out quite as well.

Once the game started, I could not articulate anything. What I was seeing on the field would not register in words. I could not remember names of guys I had shared a locker room with for an entire season. I fumbled with nearly every sentence. I don't know if I even made one bit of sense the entire game. Mike Bream carried me. I later found out that my brain had been so traumatized, my vocabulary was still limited over two months later. The truth was, it was *very* limited because it was not big in the first place.

That night I sat in my hotel room staring out the window at the Seattle skyline for two hours without a thought in my head. I was still so damaged cognitively that trying to talk for three-plus hours was not the smartest thing to do. It turned my brain to nothing.

After that game, I didn't gain much clarity about how to be a good broadcaster but I did establish one fact: I was horrible at it in my current state.

To this day I have no idea why Fox called me to do another game, but they did. It's my guess that they could not find anyone else to do it, and since it was the last game of the year they probably said, *What the heck, he can't get any worse.*

They were right. I did not get any worse—but I surely did

not get any better. Even though I didn't stay on with Fox, I had nonetheless been given a taste of the work I wanted to pursue. From there, my path ahead became clearer. I knew how to pave it, and it would be no small task.

From February to June that off-season, I continued making calls and following leads. During this time, I auditioned for some openings at ESPN. The host of my audition was Mike Tirico.

In the audition, we acted out broadcasts in real time, giving me ample opportunity to discuss the game I love and share my experience and knowledge. Mike would open the broadcasts as he does so well, laying the foundation of what he and I would be talking about. At the right moment he would then pass the floor to me and I was to do my thing. We talked about several current topics, but the one I remember most was about Bam Morris, the back the Steelers drafted when I left for Chicago. He had put on a lot of weight and it was affecting his play. Mike asked me for my thoughts and though I was nervous, I got through it. I talked for about two minutes—an eternity in broadcasting—and then handed it back to him. I didn't have any gauge for how I did.

A few weeks later, I happened to run into Tirico at the Phoenix airport. Perfect opportunity, I thought, to get some good feedback on my audition. I asked him how I did.

"Merril, you just babbled," he replied kindly but directly. "You made no sense. I'm really sorry." He then confessed ESPN was worried I was still having problems from my concussions.

They were right, and I was devastated. The drive home from the airport was a long one as my mind turned into a battlefield between thoughts of throwing in the towel and thoughts of pressing forward.

We often overlook one of the most important unseen forces at work in our lives. It is something called *momentum*. Today's opportunities were shaped by our actions in the past. What we can do tomorrow has everything to do with what we attempt and accomplish today. I believe it is impossible to determine just how significant one action will or won't be to your future. But the path to constant victory is still fairly straightforward. Fight today and you will live to fight tomorrow.

The doors of opportunity in broadcasting should not have remained open to me with two poor Fox broadcasts and a babbling ESPN interview as my measuring sticks. But while national opportunities began to pass me by, local ones still existed. I knew in my spirit that I was to stay on the path. Fortunately, my life's work to that point had created many relationships with people who wanted to see me succeed. This momentum would begin to play out.

I had never rested on my laurels. I had fought hard and had always done my part to help my team succeed. I had proven myself a trustworthy and tireless worker. As a result, despite the Fox games and my poor showing at the audition, ESPN asked me to be a color analyst for college games. I was also asked by Pittsburgh's local TV and ABC radio affiliate, WTAE, to become the first player in the booth for the Steelers game-day radio broadcast.

For the next eighteen months, I would not only get my feet wet in broadcasting, I would nearly drown in order to learn how to swim. A radio legend named Myron Cope would make sure of it.

At the time of my invitation, Cope was already an A-list celebrity in Pittsburgh for his two decades in the broadcast booth, a span during which he became the inventor of the Terrible Towel, the purveyor of the "Double Yoi!" and the creator of such sticky nicknames as "Jack Splat," "the Bus," and "Slash." When the WTAE producer called and asked me if I would like to join Cope and Bill Hillgrove in the booth, I quickly said "Yes!" then asked, "But what does Myron think?" The answer was what I expected.

He was furious and did not want it to happen—and he had every reason for his response. I had next to no experience and was nowhere near his caliber of talent. I'm sure his first thought was that I would only drag the broadcast down. In short, I didn't belong in the booth with him, but the Steelers and the WTAE executives wanted me. And besides, they said, if I didn't do it someone else would. How bad could it really be?

I was about to find out.

One thing you have to understand is that Myron Cope is still regarded today as one of the greatest sports announcers in the history of broadcasting. In 2004, he became the first pro football sportscaster to be inducted into the Radio Hall of Fame. He wasn't just a popular guy in Pittsburgh—radio personalities everywhere recognized him as one of the best. I knew going into this opportunity that a guy with Myron's experience could either make or break my career in the booth. I called him right away to let him know I considered joining him a privilege and that I would give my all.

The first bad sign was that he did not return any of my calls.

I understood he was a busy man, so I waited until I saw him at the Steelers' first 1995 preseason game in Buffalo.

I walked up to him before the game. I told him I was not there to take his job and was grateful for the opportunity. I just wanted to learn all I could from him and Bill, I said, and I would do whatever he wanted.

"This is not my idea," he replied. "Having a third guy in the booth will not work."

I completely understood where he was coming from. He had been there for almost as many years as I had been alive. This booth was his baby and he was going to put up a fight to keep it that way. I admired his sentiment. And he would put up a great fight.

I had absolutely no idea what to expect. No one had given me any direction on what to do or outlined my specific role in the broadcast. I had not even been invited to the production meeting. When the game was about to start and I made my way to the booth, I noticed there were only two chairs. For years there had been only two people in that booth, so it did not bother me that they had forgotten a chair for me. I grabbed one and put it right between Myron and Bill.

Myron's gaze conveyed only one message: *Son, wait till I get done with you.*

While the Bills and Steelers played football on the field beneath us, a tennis match ensued in the booth. I looked right when Bill talked and left when Myron talked, and the only words I could get in during the first half were "And—," "I—," or, "But—."

I could not get a sentence in to save my life, and Myron was not about to let me. I'm sure he was thinking, *The less the concussed football player speaks, the better for everyone.*

When halftime came, I stepped out of the booth and wondered how I was ever going to contribute in this situation. I reflected on how so many challenges in my life had been similar to this one. Myron and Bill were thinking about Myron and Bill. They were concentrating on giving their best. They weren't thinking about how they could include me. I was invited to do this job with them. There was an expected individual initiative that came with the invitation. It is the same with every opportunity before us.

No opportunity ends with the invitation. It is only the beginning. The next step—no matter what combination of resources is required—is always action.

I walked back into that booth and took my seat between these two professionals. The second half began and I acted.

I not only took the floor, I stepped all over Myron and Bill. I interrupted, finished their sentences, and inserted my opinions whenever and wherever I wanted. I think I saw steam billowing from Myron's ears.

The scenario continued for five weeks—them trying to carry on an entertaining broadcast and me trying to get some airtime—until I got a call from the station manager. Come in and meet with him, he said. It was then and there he let me know Myron was not happy. He was stating the obvious. Myron's nonverbal cues each week left no doubt about his opinion. The station manager then said he had spoken with Myron and Bill, and they'd written down specific descriptions for our roles in the booth. He read them to me:

1. Bill Hillgrove will be the play-by-play guy the way he always has.
2. Myron will give color to the play the way he always has.
3. Merril will speak when spoken to.

It sounded like a slap in the face, but I'm telling you I went out of that room with joy. I finally had some direction and would not have to fight for airtime.

Next game I discovered they had not only reduced my speaking role, they had also moved my chair back with the director, a tier behind Myron and Bill. I could not see the whole field unless I stood up or leaned over my table.

Myron instructed me to keep my eyes on him at all times so that when he turned around, I would be ready to respond. There was one problem. Because I was sitting one elevated row back and he was only about five foot four, he could not see over my table. His request meant I would have to lean over the table the whole game.

I did what I was asked for two games, but because I was being asked only about six questions a game, the situation was doing more to keep me from watching the game than it was to improve the broadcast. I adjusted the protocol and started to lean over when I wanted to talk and sit back when I wanted to watch the game.

At times, I would sit back and enjoy the game for an entire

quarter. Myron didn't like it. As soon as the quarter ended, he'd shoot up to my tier and let me know I was not leaning over enough.

Myron and I remained in this clumsy, painful apprenticeship for nearly a season and a half. And I was the clumsy, painful one. While I slowly improved behind the mike working both ESPN college broadcasts and the Steelers games every weekend, it is no stretch to say Myron was probably as excited as I was about the call I received around the fifth game of the 1996 regular season.

ESPN called and asked if I would like to change from doing college games to being a full-time analyst on the NFL side. As much as I respected Myron and Bill and appreciated their allowing me to stumble my way to some growth on their show, I knew they did just fine without a dumb, concussed former player in the booth. They were professionals through and through, and I barely an amateur. I needed to move on to an opportunity with a lot more room to learn and grow. I intended to see this career through, and I knew there was a short ceiling in the WTAE booth. The new ESPN opportunity had a high ceiling.

After he retired in 1989, Mark Malone started working for the NBC affiliate in Pittsburgh, covering Steelers games. He would come into our locker room after games looking for interviews. One problem was that Mark had not been the friendliest guy to the younger players during his days with the Steelers. On one particular instance, he walked up to Greg Lloyd after a home game, and Lloyd told him to get lost in not-so-uncertain terms.

Mark then proceeded to ask another player and got the same result. I was watching this unfold. Mark then walked up to me and asked for an interview. He didn't give me the time of day either when he played with the Steelers, but I didn't want to disrespect him. I gave him a good interview. He was grateful. More important, I gained Mark's respect.

Mark would go on to become one of the hosts of the *Edge NFL Matchup* show in 1993 (now the *State Farm NFL Matchup*). Three years later, one of his cohosts held out, and my name came up as a replacement option. Mark got word and told the producers, "You need to grab Merril." The timing couldn't have been better, and I was hungry to hone this new craft of mine.

One thing Greg Cosell, the show's producer, made clear in that phone call was that *Matchup* was not going to be an easy show. "You'll be working with the two hardest-working guys in the business," he asserted. He was referring to Ron "Jaws" Jaworski and Mark Malone. The thought didn't scare me one bit, but I still knew I had an uphill battle for other reasons. Not only were my skills still very raw, my cognitive abilities hadn't fully returned and I was entering a situation where I could no longer hide it.

In a radio booth, I could hide being frayed or frustrated. In a television studio, I had to constantly give off the appearance of having it all together. I was an expert analyst, expected to know, or at least look as if I knew, what I was talking about.

To accomplish this I had to spend forty to fifty hours a week studying film, taking notes, and talking to coaches in preparation for one show. The preparation wasn't without its own challenges.

The Jacksonville Jaguars were playing the Chargers on the upcoming Monday night game, and I'd left messages for Chris Palmer, the offensive coordinator, and Dick Jauron, the defensive coordinator. Dick called me back that same day, and as soon as he said hello my mind blanked. I couldn't remember if he was the offensive or defensive coordinator. I wasn't in my office where I kept my notes, so with the cordless phone to my ear I started jogging to the other side of the house. I had to say something to fill the gap and so I took a stab.

"It must be nice," I said, "to have a guy like Natrone Means on the team."

There was a pause and I knew I'd guessed wrong.

"Yeah," Dick finally replied, "I'm glad we don't have to defend him."

Embarrassed, I apologized and admitted that I was having trouble remembering who did what with each team every week. Dick was gracious, but I knew if this sort of thing continued, I wouldn't last long in this job. I had to find a way to succeed despite the brain damage I still suffered.

To avoid a similar mishap on television, I had to memorize each word I was going to say. I was so worried about messing up I didn't sleep the night before a show. I would stand in the hotel bathroom all night reciting my lines over and over in front of the mirror. I did this for almost two years.

When the tape was rolling I couldn't compute anything my cohosts were saying to me or I'd immediately forget what I had memorized. Even if one of them hotly disputed a point I just made, I still picked up my script where I left off without addressing the dispute. My brain couldn't hold on to my script and enter into a conversation at the same time.

And despite my intense memorization, I also fumbled through my lines far more than the others. In fact, I never saw Mark or Jaws make mistakes. What helped me those early months was an overabundance of grace. Mark and Jaws knew I was struggling and they never got frustrated when I messed up. "Don't worry about it, Merril," they would say. "Take your time." Their encouragement took a lot of pressure off me because I knew they had busy schedules and things to get done.

At one point, Greg came to me before a taping and suggested giving him a few keywords about what I wanted to say. He then created cue cards for me that he would hold beneath the camera. Those often saved me and allowed me to begin to relax in front of the camera.

The truth is that my personality didn't come out on ESPN until my third year. During the first two years, it took everything in me to avoid making a fool of myself. My mind wasn't restored, and it became clear early on that outworking everyone else was my only way to stay in the game. I'm convinced that my work ethic—the fact that everyone at ESPN knew I was giving it everything I could to succeed—was what kept me there when I wasn't progressing as quickly as I should have been.

That, and a great man named Gerry Matalon.

During those early years in the ESPN studio, I gave all I could give to becoming a good analyst and he knew it. He knew how bad I wanted to succeed and how difficult a challenge it was for me. Every slow step of the way, Gerry was my best broadcasting coach and my best fan.

Gerry was my first producer at ESPN, but he ended up being more than a producer. He was the first person to challenge me to let my personality come through on TV. One day, just before a show, he was watching me interact with a friend. The two of us were reviewing some highlights we were going to show and I was having fun. I was giving all kinds of energy toward my commentary, and I was very animated. After a few minutes of observing this, Gerry came over to me and said, "Merril, you're funny. You have a quick wit and I saw an energy in you just now that I never see on TV.

"You need to be more like that on TV," he continued. "Be you."

He then gave a piece of advice I still recite to this day.

"Every time you go on TV, I want you to think, 'Be bold and dynamic.'"

While it might sound like fairly basic advice, to me it was gold because I had no clue what I was doing. I only knew I wanted to be a broadcaster but had no idea how to do it well.

On the field of play, succeeding was pretty straightforward. To make the team and continue playing, I had to be better at running the ball. I had to block better than the other guys at my position. I had to catch better. I had to know the plays and be a playmaker.

Succeeding in broadcasting, especially on TV, plays out differently. The primary forces are controlled and time-sensitive. A Hall of Fame career on the football field may earn you an opportunity in broadcasting, but if you can't find a way to recalibrate all the fierce skill, intellect, and will you displayed on the field into poise, poignancy, and wit, you won't make it. It's a misconception that any NFL player who feels like it can jump from the field into the studio. The truth is that the jump is a giant leap, and far more miss it than make it—especially at ESPN. It hasn't remained an award-winning network by fielding anything less than excellence.

Without a producer like Gerry Matalon, I don't know that I would have made the leap. To say it was a leap of faith on my part is true. There were things outside my control that I'm convinced only God could have orchestrated. Case in point was Gerry's assignment to me and personal interest in me. Perhaps the bigger leap of faith is better ascribed to Gerry. In those early days when I was prone to, in the words of Mike Tirico, "babble," Gerry kept reminding me to be my bold and dynamic self. He was convinced of something in me I could not yet see myself.

With the words "BE BOLD AND DYNAMIC" handwritten at the top of every page of notes in every broadcast, I eventually began to deliver analysis with greater authority and clarity, despite my cognitive dysfunction. What I did not expect was that Gerry's impact on me reached outside the walls of the studio.

Because he was interested in me as a family man as well as an NFL analyst, he was a constant reminder that there was more to my life's work than a job.

It was no coincidence that one day at ESPN's Bristol, Connecticut, headquarters, Gerry handed me a book, Dale Carnegie's *How to Win Friends and Influence People*. I opened to page one on my return flight to Arizona, where my family then lived. By page 14, I had come across a story that has never left me for more reasons than one. It is called "Father Forgets," written by W. Livingston Larned and originally published as an editorial in *People's Home Journal:*

Listen, son: I am saying this as you lie asleep, one little paw crumpled under your cheek and the blond curls stickily wet on your damp forehead. I have stolen into your room alone. Just a few minutes ago, as I sat reading my paper in the library, a stifling wave of remorse swept over me. Guiltily I came to your bedside.

There are the things I was thinking, son: I had been cross to you. I scolded you as you were dressing for school because you gave your face merely a dab with a towel. I took you to task for not cleaning your shoes. I called out angrily when you threw some of your things on the floor.

At breakfast I found fault, too. You spilled things. You gulped down your food. You put your elbows on the table. You spread butter too thick on your bread. And as you started off to play and I made for my train, you turned and waved a hand and called, "Goodbye, Daddy!" and I frowned, and said in reply, "Hold your shoulders back!"

Then it began all over again in the late afternoon. As I came up the road I spied you, down on your knees, playing marbles. There were holes in your stockings. I humiliated you before your boyfriends by marching you ahead of me to the house. Stockings were

172

expensive—and if you had to buy them you would be more careful! Imagine that, son, from a father!

Do you remember, later, when I was reading in the library, how you came in timidly, with a sort of hurt look in your eyes? When I glanced up over my paper, impatient at the interruption, you hesitated at the door. "What is it you want?" I snapped.

You said nothing, but ran across in one tempestuous plunge, and threw your arms around my neck and kissed me, and your small arms tightened with an affection that God had set blooming in your heart and which even neglect could not wither. And then you were gone, pattering up the stairs.

Well, son, it was shortly afterwards that my paper slipped from my hands and a terrible sickening fear came over me. What has habit been doing to me? The habit of finding fault, of reprimanding—this was my reward to you for being a boy. It was not that I did not love you; it was that I expected too much of youth. I was measuring you by the yardstick of my own years.

And there was so much that was good and fine and true in your character. The little heart of you was as big as the dawn itself over the wide hills. This was shown by your spontaneous impulse to rush in and kiss me good night. Nothing else matters tonight, son. I have come to your bedside in the darkness, and I have knelt there, ashamed!

It is a feeble atonement; I know you would not understand these things if I told them to you during your waking hours. But tomorrow I will be a real daddy! I will chum with you, and suffer when you suffer, and laugh when you laugh. I will bite my tongue when impatient words come. I will keep saying as if it were a ritual: "He is nothing but a boy—a little boy!"

I am afraid I have visualized you as a man. Yet as I see you now, son, crumpled and weary in your cot, I see that you are still a baby. Yesterday you were in your mother's arms, your head on her shoulder. I have asked too much, too much.[1]

As I read this father's letter to his son, a sea of emotions swept over me. I was suddenly the little boy in that letter but without the father's love, acceptance, or apology. I started to sob from a depth in my soul I did not know existed. I sobbed until there were no more tears to cry. I then let it all go—all the things my father had done to me, and all that he had not done. And I forgave him.

My next thought was of my own fatherhood. As a young dad I was always trying to find a way to improve. I had been asking myself, *How can I best teach my kids to make good decisions in life?* What better guidance than to measure them with the yardsticks of their own years, not mine? This advice gave me the patience and perspective to properly love and teach Kori and Beau to find a way through life's challenges.

Equipping my children to be strong, wise, and resourceful and then fiercely follow their dreams is something I found a way to learn outside my home. Like my father, hard work has always been a high value. A dark sky was his regular morning companion, and it has been mine as well. But I also learned from other men how to turn my hard work into a life's work. Chuck Noll made it important to me. Gerry Matalon reminded me how.

I was never more grateful for that book's reminder when just a few years later, while in confident stride in my ESPN career, I learned I had cancer.

My father called when he heard the news. We hadn't spoken in seven years—since he told me he needed to focus on his new family.

His first words were an attempt to reconcile his shortcomings as a father.

"I know I didn't do everything right," he said, "but I did the best I could with what I knew."

It wasn't the first time he said it, but a part of me knew it would be the last time I heard it. Besides, there was more truth in his statement than he knew. He did do the best he could with what he knew. His great failure is that he never found a way to know more.

I accepted his apology. I had already forgiven him.

We said good-bye and returned to our separate lives.

9

Finding a Way to Live

A few weeks before the conversation with my father, I fielded the call from Dr. Marks confirming I had cancer and a minimum of six months of chemo in front of me.

"There are no guarantees it will work," he said.

I was numb. I sat down on a bed for a few minutes to try and digest the harsh reality of the news. It was so hard to believe I had cancer.

I often hear people ask what you would do if you were told you were dying. I now know there is no way to imagine those emotions until you are there. I had thought about it before that day at my family's Idaho cabin. I had wondered what I would do and how I would feel. I never came close to drumming up the emotions, fears, and thoughts that surfaced when I knew for sure I had cancer.

The closest comparison I had was the sting of death I experienced when my mom died. I felt firsthand the jarring alterations that occur after a loved one's death. I felt the loneliness, the heartache, and the confusion. I witnessed the gaping wound it made in my family—a wound that never fully healed and ultimately tore our family apart.

As similar feelings arose and elevated a level higher than before, my one prevailing thought was that my children could not feel this way. They could not go through what I went through when I was young. They could not feel this loneliness, confusion, and great heartache. My family could not be broken.

I did not want them to see their father die.

The first reeling visual that popped into my head as I sat there on the bed was the movie *Dying Young*. It was my only experience with the effects of cancer. While I had seen bald people who were obviously going through treatment, I had never known anyone going through it. I had never talked with someone with cancer. I had also never witnessed the battle from beginning to end. My only reference was that two-hour movie. I had no clue of the advancements that important companies like Genentech had made, so I was trying to prepare myself to deal with, and my children to endure, what I had seen Campbell Scott suffer through.

Baldness. Emaciation. Increasing weakness. Tragedy.

As I gathered my thoughts and descended those cabin stairs, I looked at Kori and Beau and thought, *They are so innocent. Why do they have to deal with this at such a young age?*

I then went through with the telling and, with only a moment's pause, all I found a way to possess and all I found a way to impart came rushing back to me in the form of a blond-haired, blue-eyed whisper: "Daddy, you're just gonna have to find a way."

More happened in that moment than a passionate decision to defeat the disease. I was seeing tangible evidence that my three decades of resourcefulness had become a life's work. The realization was everything I needed to keep fighting and find a way to continue living.

I love being a dad, and every morning when I woke with cancer I gave thanks that I was fighting the battle and my children weren't. There is no question cancer was the toughest challenge of my life, but I don't know how I would have handled myself if Kori or Beau was suffering with the disease. I am always in awe of those amazing parents who have children with cancer. They possess resources unknown to someone who has not stood in their shoes. Children are God's greatest gifts to us, and there is nothing more heart-wrenching and unnatural than to see them suffering.

Even though I was the one with the disease, I vowed to keep the worst to myself and protect Kori and Beau from as much distress as possible.

One way I did this was by keeping a commitment I made when they were very young. I promised myself that if they asked me to play with or talk to them, I would drop what I was doing and be with them—no matter what.

Early on in their lives, I came to the realization that when kids need you they are rarely asking for all day. What they are asking for, the vast majority of the time, is a few minutes—especially when they are little.

When Kori and Beau were maybe three and five, and they wanted me to play with them, I used to time how long we were together. It nearly always lasted between five and ten minutes. I knew I was crazy not to give them that time. The return is so disproportionately high on the investment it can't be calculated.

I embodied this same philosophy all the way through my chemo.

One day, when I was halfway done with my treatment and very worn down, Kori and Beau asked if I would come jump on the trampoline. They love it when I can help them "double jump" and get some serious air. I made my way to the backyard.

It was a bittersweet few minutes. Once again, I found myself asking, *If I am not here, who will do this with them? Who will they ask to double jump them if I'm gone?*

I was deploying my plan to beat the living tar out of cancer, but what if it wasn't enough? Such questions did not overwhelm my mind but they were always there, especially in sweet moments like when we were on the trampoline.

Yet when the chemo began to manifest itself outwardly, the reality of both sides of the battle became more evident. Finding a way to live meant, first and foremost, keeping perspective. I would need help.

In that dreadful phone call at the cabin, Dr. Marks had told me to shave my head, "because after your first treatment, you will start losing your hair." Seventeen days after my first treatment I had yet to see any signs this would happen.

Then I was warming up to play a game of basketball in my YMCA league. I brushed my hair from my eyes because I had started to sweat. I returned my hand to the ball and a tassel of hair was woven between my fingers. I went ice cold. I reached up and grabbed some hair between my index finger and thumb. I pulled and felt nothing. Then I looked. Between my two fingers was a tuft of hair, like grass I'd yanked from the front lawn.

I was shocked. I had recovered so well after my first treatment I thought I would not lose my hair. In fact, I checked my pillow every day and watched the drain in the shower. Ten days after my first treatment I had not seen a single hair fall out. I thought I would fall into that small percentage of people who actually keep their hair.

Clearly I was not part of that rare group. As I stood there on the court, I could not help myself. I kept reaching up to my head and pulling out more hair. I didn't want to believe it was real.

One of my teammates noticed me standing there picking at my head. He came over and asked what was wrong.

"Grab some of my hair and pull," I told him.

He did, and the look on his face mirrored how I felt. He looked at me, then my hair, then at the chunk of my hair in his hand.

"Did that hurt?"

"I didn't feel a thing."

You've no doubt heard someone exclaim they are so frustrated they are pulling their hair out. What ensued during that game was not about frustration, but the phrase was more than a pun. I was literally pulling my hair out the entire game, and once my teammates realized what was going on everyone wanted a turn. My head was like a dipping tray. It is a wonder I had any hair left after the game. It would not have mattered because I knew what I needed to do next. I had been putting it off as long as I could. Now, it was a foregone conclusion.

Often when a person has been diagnosed with cancer, people do not know what to say or do. I was in that category just a few weeks earlier, so I told people who found out that it was okay to just come up and say, "I don't know what to say, but I'm here for you and I will be praying for you."

I was very fortunate that the community I live in is full of people who took me at my word. Many of them, in fact, went a step further.

Our coach for the YMCA basketball team was Tom Pendery. When he and another longtime friend of ours named Jim Head knew I was going to shave my head after that game, they came to me and said, "We're going to do it with you."

We immediately caravanned to my house, where we took care of business one head after another. My son, Beau, heard what was going on, and he and his buddies joined in, too. While the act itself was nothing other cancer patients' friends had not done before, their act of camaraderie touched me and made losing my hair so much easier. When you are going through such a gruesome disease, the little touches of kindness and caring make a big difference.

I went from playing in a basketball game with a full head of hair to Mr. Clean in less than two hours. I remember looking in the mirror at what once was one of my ongoing worries. I was bald. And now I had a stark and constant reminder of the cancer inside me.

One thing I did when Dr. Marks told me I was going to go bald was that I immediately put a plan together to hide it. I called two friends from my Steelers playing days—equipment manager Rodgers Freyvogel and former PR associate Pat Hanlon, who was now the Giants' head PR guy—and I asked them each to send me a dozen skullcaps. I also went online and bought a few more. The skullcaps had been sitting in a box. Now, I had to pull them out and begin using them.

One incident finally woke me up and gave me proper perspective.

Where my work was concerned, I had been worried sick that I was going to be doing live coverage of the NFL draft on ESPN. When I started the chemo and nothing happened for two weeks, I stopped worrying. But once early April hit and I didn't have a thread of hair on my head, I was suddenly mortified of being bald on television. I racked my brain on how I could hide my head for two full days. I knew I couldn't wear the skullcaps, so I came up with another plan.

I called Eddie White and Tom Shine of Reebok and asked if I could have a hat for every NFL team. I would wear the hat of the team that was on the clock each time I was on TV. I had only one more hurdle to overcome: I had to get ESPN's approval.

I called Jay Rothman, who was producing the draft and who has always been a great friend to me, and I asked for his approval.

"If that's what you want to do," he said, "then sure. But

when you get to New York the day before the draft, I want to do dinner."

I said of course and when I arrived the day before the draft, all the ESPN guys had a ten-hour preparation meeting. Jay and I then went to dinner.

We talked briefly about the draft and placed our orders. He then looked across the table at me with steady eyes.

"Merril," he said, "what are you hiding?"

"What do you mean?"

"It's your call," he explained, "but I think you would be making a huge mistake to wear those hats for the next two days. You're not the only one that has cancer right now, and you didn't ask for this, and you did nothing to deserve this. Go out there the next two days and show people that you're not going to back down or hide from this."

His words changed my perspective from that day forward. I would hide nothing except the physical pain I was going through. I would hold my bald head up high and display my battle scars so that others would be encouraged.

I went on air the next two days with only the stylist's makeup on my head to dim the sheen. I was never again embarrassed by my baldness. In fact, I soon learned that losing my hair was a sign that the chemo was working.

Hair is a fast-growing cell just like a cancer cell, and the chemo they push into your body is attracted to fast-growing cells. My baldness made it clear the chemo was in my system and had killed my hair. I prayed it was also killing the cancer.

I would eventually begin to see signs it was.

It was estimated I had a two- to three-pound tumor behind my stomach that reached down to my lower back. What I did not realize before my diagnosis was that the size of the tumor was slowly taking away my abdominal flexibility. When I slid into my car, I would often hit my head on the edge of the roof. When I pulled into traffic, I just could not turn my head to see what was coming behind me. I would have to lift myself up on the seat and completely turn my entire body. I had also noticed that when I worked out, I would have a funny taste in my mouth. However, because the changes were so subtle and occurred over time, they didn't set off an alarm. It wasn't until after my first treatment that I realized how much the tumor had begun to take over my body.

Before my first treatment, I had several doctor visits where the primary focus was explaining and outlining what was going to take place. A major piece of that puzzle was the type of chemotherapy doctors were going to use. I knew all of it was poison and extremely powerful, but I wanted to know what was going into me and how I could best prepare my body for it.

I was told that my treatment was known by the acronym CHOP. It stood for the four drugs that would be administered separately but work in sync to attack the cancer: cyclophosphamide (represented by the C in the acronym); Adriamycin, which has the brand name of Hydroxydoxorubicin (and represents the H in the acronym); vincristine, which goes by the brand name Oncovin (and is represented by the O); and the drug prednisone (represented by the P). CHOP is typically administered for a total of six cycles, one every four weeks, for a total of approximately five to six months.

I was then told there would be a fifth drug called Rituxan that was fairly new. In November 1997, its creator, Genentech, made it the first therapeutic antibody approved for treating cancer in the United States. It was the one drug of them all that gave me added hope.

I did some thorough research and discovered that statistics showed Rituxan had frequently helped improve the success of chemotherapy treatments. While it was still being used on a trial basis to treat non-Hodgkin's lymphoma in 2003, and while administering it made my chemo day eight grueling hours instead of six, I felt it was worth it.

When I walked into the treatment room for the first time, I was hopeful and as prepared as I could be. One question I did not yet have an answer for was how fast the drugs would work. I had not thought to ask until that point.

When the doctor administering my treatment walked in, that was my first question.

He looked at me with confidence and said, "Seconds."

"Seconds?"

"Yes, in seconds."

I couldn't confirm that anything was happening while I sat in the recliner all day, but as soon as I went to step into my car, I understood how powerful and immediate the drugs' effects were. When I slid into my seat, I just about shot myself through the other side. The treatment hit the tumor so hard my flexibility had fully returned. I could duck with ease and turn as I once had.

I drove to my basketball game, and as soon as I arrived I tested myself on the court.

I grabbed a ball and started dribbling up and down the court. I could bend, twist, and cut so effortlessly, I was amazed I hadn't noticed the limitations the tumor had been inflicting on me. The doctors believed the tumor had been growing for nine or ten months before we discovered it. There was a lot to undo.

For my part, attacking this nasty tumor meant continuing to do all the things I loved and was used to doing. I continued running, lifting weights, and playing basketball. One of my other theories was to make great gains in adding lean muscle mass and trimming fat. I knew I needed physical strength as much as emotional and mental strength. I ate to perfection and never missed a workout.

But I believe one of the greatest advantages I gave myself came about when I experienced the CHOP and Rituxan working in seconds. I'd always been a proponent of drinking a lot of water, but when I realized that each round of chemo poison was effectively done in a matter of minutes, water became my most important ally.

I figured I had some two thousand pores in my face alone. So why not use every pore in my body to rid myself of the awful effects of the chemo? My plan was to turn over one gallon of water every twenty-four hours. This was particularly important on treatment days.

I would rise at seven a.m. to work out and then head to treatment where, for the next eight hours, toxins would invade the cancer in my body. Immediately following treatment, I would head to the Y and play basketball, letting the sweat drip the poison from my pores. The following day I would almost feel normal. I was no longer toxic.

This by no means meant I did not have my share of difficult days. Some were related to the physical effects of the chemo. Others were related to my chemo-induced limitations.

Despite my rigid routine, the drugs eventually built up in my system and broke down cells in my body besides the cancer. About three months into my treatment, I started to get tingling in my fingers. My nerves were beginning to misfire.

I also had what looked like burn marks on my back. It appeared the chemo had burned through my skin. This is one reason you are told to stay out of sunlight when going through chemo. I found this out two days before my family was going to the beach on spring break.

I knew I did not need to do anything to further harm my body, so I had to forgo playing in the sand with Kori and Beau during the heat of the day. While they bodysurfed and swam in the ocean, I sat inside the beach house watching hours of tape on the top college prospects.

After my fourth month of treatment, I had another bitter-sweet moment. This time I was alone.

I knew going into chemotherapy that I would have six rounds, one every three to four weeks, and that we would do a scan after my fourth round. I made up my mind that I would be cancer-free after the fourth month.

After receiving my four-month scan and heading home, I got a call from Dr. Marks. I was ready to hear the good news.

Dr. Marks confirmed what I was waiting to hear. The scan showed no sign of the tumor.

"Thank you so much for all you've done for me," I said to him. "I'm so glad I am done with chemo."

The silence on the other end was not a good sign.

"Merril," he finally replied, "that's not a good idea. Just because the scans are clean doesn't mean you are done with treatment. For your best chances at being cured, you need to finish."

He paused again. I didn't know what to say.

"I can't make you finish," he then confessed. "That is your call."

I was devastated but completely understood. When I left that treatment center earlier that day, I was confident I would never return. Now I was looking at returning two more times over two months.

While I could have chosen to move back into normal life, I knew Dr. Marks was far wiser and more knowledgeable than I was. I would finish my last two treatments, even though I knew the tumor was gone.

It was during these last two months I experienced the worst effects of chemo.

After the first three treatments, I would always allow myself what I called a crash day. Since the prednisone kept me wired for five days, around day eight I would run out of gas. This would be my day of rest.

However, after my fourth treatment, day eight fell on a

day I had committed to go on a field trip with Beau. I kept my commitment.

We took a bus to a science museum. On the ride, keeping my eyes open was getting harder by the minute. We then toured the museum for a while. I thought of a Road Runner episode where the coyote pried his eyes open with toothpicks. I was there.

The next thing I heard was the best news of the day. We were headed into a theater to watch a 3D film that was twenty minutes long. I immediately thought of taking a power nap.

As Beau watched the video with his classmates, I found a bench in the museum hallway and took a much-needed nap.

I woke a little disoriented. I felt as if I had slept a long time.

Unfortunately, I had.

It is usually the kids who go missing in such scenarios, but this time it was the parent. I had fallen so fast asleep, in an area where no one could see me, I had missed the bus ride home. I had to call a friend to come get me.

Once home, I drove to school to make sure Beau was okay. He was fine, and the office said they figured I did not feel well and had left the museum on my own.

After treatments five and six, I fared no better. While the two crash days fell on days I had no museum trips, the chemo was breaking my body down further. It no longer had a three-pound tumor to target. The drugs were killing healthy cells.

Charlie LaVallee, one of the great men in my life who spear-headed the Highmark Caring Foundation, for which I am the Chairman, suggested I video my last treatment. Frankly, I just wanted to get through the last treatment without incident. I could not understand the value in filming it, even though I agreed to do it. I even joked, "You trying to document my death?"

My last treatment was by far the worst. I had to ask the nurses to stop several times as I could literally feel my tissue being shredded inside me. I willed my way to the end and then immediately went home, worked out, and started looking for hair growth.

The video of that day is priceless. Instead of mere words, I can now show people suffering with cancer what I went through and encourage them to find a way to fight through it. For this reason, my final day of chemo was both my most difficult day and my most valuable day for helping others. That matters now as much as anything. "The proof of gold," wrote Benjamin Franklin, "is fire." I was glad I chose to endure the fire.

There were many challenges along the path to my cure, especially at the end. While Kori and Beau were my constant source of motivation, what surprised me with extra boosts of strength each day were the cards, letters, and e-mails that constantly poured in. There were also the phone calls from people who would simply say, "Merril, I was thinking of you. I don't know what to say, but I want you to know you are in my prayers." My dear friend, Wilson Hoyle, did this on a daily basis.

Throughout my football career, I trained by myself. I was no maverick; I was just always better at motivating myself than others were. Even after the NFL, I rarely trained with another person. But during my bout with cancer, that changed. I learned I needed others to win the most difficult battles.

During chemo, a friend in my neighborhood named Dave Otto drove to my house every day to work out with me. It did not matter what time or what day—he was always there. His presence provided a huge lift to me. It carried me through many days during that year.

In the summer of 2003, when I was officially cancer- and chemo-free, one of my business partners, Bill Newman, threw a party for me. He rented out a building and had T-shirts printed that read: "Hoge Cancer Free 2003!"

Everyone in my neighborhood showed up, including people I had never met who had been praying for me and sending cards and thoughtful gifts along the way. Such acts of service and kindness still warm my heart and remind me that life is about so much more than me.

Victories are found in different ways. Some are found merely from the application of great skill. Such victories are common.

Other victories are found when sharp intellect is added to great skill—brains *and* brawn. Such victories are less common than those found by skill alone, but they are not uncommon.

There are still less common victories found in a rare combination of skill, intellect, and passion-fueled will. These encapsulate what it means to be uncommon on the field of battle. While the powerful combination is available to everyone, few apply it consistently enough to see their dreams unfold into reality. Those who find a way to live out their dreams tap into every resource available to them.

Yet the rarest victory of all is found when the uncommon combination of skill, intellect, and will is required but not enough; when victory requires something outside your control.

This is when faith becomes necessary. And when faith is involved, victory doesn't always look the way you think it will.

One of the primary reasons I wanted to play in the NFL was so I could stand in the players' tunnel on Super Bowl Sunday and hear the announcer say, "And now...in his fourth year at fullback...number thirty-three...Merril Hoge!"

I would then play the game of my life, and we would become the Super Bowl champions. When I was young I would play it out in my head that the Super Bowl would fall on my birthday, January 26. It never worked out the way I imagined.

I had two of the greatest back-to-back playoff games in Steelers history—over three hundred total yards—but it was not enough for our team to reach the Super Bowl. When I reflect back on those rare moments I had in the playoffs, one thing is always very clear. I did all I could to make that dream happen. But what makes football such a great game is that it is the ultimate team sport. No player can find a way to a Super Bowl victory alone.

In the end, the Steelers teams I played for were not good enough. But I live in peace knowing I found a way to do my part to the highest degree. The greatest confirmation of this I ever received was relayed to me by a close friend of Walter Payton who was with Sweetness often in the final weeks of his life.

One day they struck up a conversation about the players Payton loved watching after he retired in 1987.

I was on his short list.

There are always cynics and excuse makers who will say victory is ultimately a matter of fate. That dreams are like lottery balls in a spinning barrel. Sometimes they spill out in your favor. Sometimes not.

There is nothing further from the truth.

There are specific reasons certain people find victory more than others. And then there is a different set of reasons I do not profess to entirely understand, in which victory is outside the realm of individual control. It is in this place that skill, intellect, and will must still be applied. And with them, faith.

Faith in those things outside your control. Faith that if God desires it to be, he will provide the additional resources you do not possess: the right people, the right timing, and the right opportunities.

Ultimately, I could not find a way around my father's abuse—but I found a way despite it. I could not find a way around my premature retirement—but I found a way beyond it. I could not find a way around cancer—but I found a way through it.

It is through faith that we come to see that certain victories cannot be found except on the other side of disappointment, pain, and adversity. The outcomes in my life that I could not control gave me the intangible tools I could not do without: resourcefulness, interdependence, and selflessness. In no other area of my life has this proven truer than in my life's work as a parent.

10

Living Your Life's Work

I loved playing football at every level. I am passionate about my work at ESPN. But the job I cherish most in my life is being a dad. It is the most important work I do.

The irony is that I never really thought about having kids when Toni and I got married. Frankly, I was not anxious to become a dad. That all changed at Kori's birth.

During the delivery, the umbilical cord got wrapped around her neck. The more Toni pushed, the more distressed Kori's breathing got. The obstetrician made the quick decision to perform an emergency C-section.

I was supposed to move away from my girls in order to give them room to work, but I stayed put. I was going to keep an eye on my wife and firstborn baby.

Fortunately, the procedure went perfectly. As they held Kori up, I noticed her fingers first. They looked like my mom's, long, elegant, and beautiful. As I studied them and then my baby's face and tiny body, an overwhelming sensation came over me. I was her daddy, and I would die for that precious little girl.

She was so fragile and helpless, and the more the nurse poked in her eyes and mouth, the more I wanted to knock the lady down like a bowling pin. Her actions seemed too rough and I didn't like it. Finally I had enough. I blurted out, "Could you please be a little more gentle?"

"This is not hurting her," she confidently replied. "We need to do these things so she can see and breathe normally."

"Okay," I said. But I still didn't like it.

When you look at a newborn baby and see how dependent she is for everything she needs to live, it is nearly impossible to not want to be a good parent. In fact, being a good parent is fairly straightforward when all it requires are objective tasks like changing diapers and holding a bottle. The real challenges come when a child's dependence includes ungratefulness and obstinacy. It doesn't take long for them to get there.

I still remember the first time I battled these traits in Kori, because the result was a lesson I have never forgotten. She was three years old.

I was in a rush to get to an important appointment and Kori had to go with me. We got to my truck, and she made it clear she was not about to sit in her car seat. I had no choice but to take her because I was the only one home, so I tried to put her in again and again, with increasing impatience. She bucked and arched her back and then finally she began crying. I struggled against her will to pull the safety strap over her and she did all she could to stop me.

Finally, my frustration reached its limit. I grabbed Kori by her shoulders and firmly pushed her into place. Immediately, she stopped fighting and got silent. She then gave me a look I still remember.

It said, *Why, Daddy?*

I was sick inside as I immediately reflected on the book I had just been given by Gerry Matalon and the story about measuring kids by the yardsticks of their own years. More important, I realized that the only thing that would break the chain of my father's abuse, and his father's abuse, was my behavior in moments just like that one. In such moments, I could either break the chain or pass it on again.

I knew I could justify forcing Kori into the seat. I was late for an appointment I could not miss and I was, after all, the boss. While I believe in the importance of structure and following through with consequences when rules are broken, I knew I had to do much better than win battles by force. I made the decision to become a teacher.

Instead of merely telling Kori she needed to sit still and then squashing her into the seat when she didn't, I vowed to teach her why it was so important that she sit in that seat. Nothing complicated. Just a firm explanation that her seat was the only thing that would keep her from getting hurt. And Daddy didn't want his little angel to ever get hurt.

When a child is still very young, this can obviously take some time to really set in, but eventually it pays big dividends.

As I peered into those sad, baby blue eyes that day in the truck, I told Kori I was wrong. While many years have passed since then—and I have had many more opportunities to make the same mistakes my father made—my confession to Kori that day sealed the deal. I never used a forceful hand on her again.

The main reason might sound very simple. For me it has been profound. As I look at my kids I can't help but see myself as a child. When I was their age, I always wanted my parents to hug me and tell me they loved me and that they were proud of me. I craved it but never received it. I didn't want my kids to feel that void in their lives for one single day.

I never realized how important this endeavor was until I made an appointment with a well-known counselor named Carol Tuttle, whose book, *Remembering Wholeness*, I had just read.

I loved her ideas on the power of the mind to heal, and I had told her I wanted to learn more. As we sat down in her office, I was taken back when she started asking me about my childhood.

"When was the last time your mother gave you a hug?" she asked.

I told her she died when I was in college.

"When she was alive, did she hug you?"

I had to really think hard. I could not remember a time that she hugged me. Still, I told her I know my mom loved me, but out of four boys I was the one who butted heads with her the most.

She then asked about my dad. "Is he still alive?"

"Yes," I said, "but I have not seen or spoken to him in almost eight years." I then explained the circumstances in which my father remarried and shifted to his new family.

"When was the last time he hugged you and told you he loved you?" she asked.

I told her he never had.

She looked straight at me. "Do you have kids?"

"Yes," I said. "Two."

She had this very interesting look on her face. "When was the last time you hugged your kids and told them you loved them?"

I looked at my watch and it was 10:10 a.m.

"I walked out my door around nine-thirty and I did that about two or three times to each of them before I left. I do that every morning and throughout every day."

"How do you know to do that?" she asked.

"I don't know how I could not do that," I replied.

She nodded and smiled, and I immediately understood that what I had accomplished and was continuing to accomplish as a parent was a momentous, ongoing victory.

I have always felt that I am my kids' time machine. I know what is ahead of them—the temptations and the challenges—and I know what skills they will need to make good decisions. My job is to equip them with that resourcefulness by getting them involved in the decision-making process and then holding them accountable for what they decide.

A good example is the day Beau was playing basketball out back, and it was time for dinner. I opened the door and called out, "Okay, Beau, make one more shot and come in."

Five minutes later and Beau had not come in. I stood outside this time.

"Beau," I called again, "I told you to come in."

"No," he fired back, "you said make one more shot before I come in and I can't make this shot."

Well, Beau was five at the time and he was trying to make, of all shots, a three-pointer.

"I said just make another shot. I didn't mean you had to make a three-pointer."

He was beside himself after that, and I could see that he was not going to come inside until he made that shot.

I walked out to the basketball court. Beau was crying.

"Son," I said, "what's wrong?"

"I can't make this stupid shot," he moaned. "I can't even get the ball there."

There was my cue.

I could have easily reminded Beau he was only five years old and a three-pointer was a very difficult shot for a five-year old, but instead I used it as a chance to hone his resourcefulness and decision-making skills.

"Well," I said, "what can you do to get stronger so you can make this shot?"

He looked up at me, wiped his eyes, and said, "I could practice with those weighted balls in your weight room for thirty minutes every day."

It was a great idea and I told him so. As we walked back inside, we promised to begin the next day. And we did. Before long, he was making the three-pointer.

What I loved most about his suggestion was that I had never thought about his practicing with the weighted ball in my weight room. Time and again, kids will surprise you if you give them the chance. So often the hurried pace in which we live can be the biggest detriment to parenting well. Many parents make the mistake of substituting telling for teaching because they believe there just isn't time to explain. I've learned nothing can replace the lessons you teach your children, through your actions and through the actions you invite them into. This doesn't change as they grow older.

Kori is now driving herself to school and Beau is not far behind, but I still work hard to maintain a tight bond with them. One thing that has always kept me close to my kids is holding hands.

I love it when they ask me to take them somewhere, anywhere. I love it because as soon as we get in the car, I turn off the radio and reach across the console to take Kori or Beau's hand in mine. I have been doing this since they could stand, so even today it does not seem weird to them. In fact, often they will grab my hand before I grab theirs. And as we hold hands we simply talk about their day and about what is going on in their lives.

These days I drive them places far less often than I used to. So when the rare occasion arises, I don't hesitate. I hop in the car and then drive as slowly as possible. Where we live, everything is nearby and most drives take less then ten minutes. It's not a lot of time, but I've learned I can live a lot of life in a matter of a few minutes like those.

For this reason, when I look back on my life and consider the things that did and did not happen, there is no doubt I would still trade a Super Bowl ring for the chance to enjoy two greater victories: beating cancer and becoming a great father. A Super Bowl ring is a great work. Securing a worthwhile legacy is a life's work. I am grateful that work continues today.

I now see that the three simple words I pinned to my corkboard wall in 1978 were far more meaningful than I could have ever known.

They not only paved a rare path before me; they saved my life.

Notes

Chapter 2. What Makes a Winner

1. According to the NFL Players Association website: www .nflplayers.com/About-us/FAQs/NFL-Hopeful-FAQS/.

Chapter 3. Attitude Is Not Enough

1. Kellee Van Keuren, "Super Trophy: The NFL's Highest Award Is a Sterling Success," *Recognition Review* 19, no. 2, February 1998.
2. According to the NFL Players Association website: www .nflplayers.com/About-us/FAQs/NFL-Hopeful-FAQs/.

Chapter 4. Uncommon Effort

1. Television announcer Curt Gowdy on the original December 23, 1972, NBC broadcast: www.youtube.com/watch?v=7xMD IcsUMmA&feature=related.
2. "Noll's Steelers Return to Blue-Collar Style; But Malone Remains Ineffective," *Washington Post*, September 15, 1987.
3. Don R. Smith, "Chuck Noll," in *The Coffin Corner* 15, no. 2, 1993.
4. The quote is attributed to Chuck Noll during a postgame press conference after a Steelers' loss.
5. Smith, "Chuck Noll."

Chapter 5. The Mind Fuels the Body

1. This was an award given each year by the Maxwell Football Club from 1989 to 2006 for the most outstanding coach in professional football.
2. http://www.who.int/mental_health/management/depression/definition/en/.
3. Alejandro Bodipo-Memba, "Life after the NFL: Typically a Struggle," *USA Today,* January 28, 2006.

Chapter 6. Passion and the Prima Donna Syndrome

1. Rick Morrissey, "In NFL, It's Better to Receive\Records Fall as Rules, Offenses Change to Make Wideouts Stars of '90s," *Rocky Mountain News*, January 28, 1996.
2. "Report says Bears lost $1.7 million in '87," *Chicago Sun-Times*, January 25, 1988, Courtesy of HighBeam Research, December 16, 2009, http://www.highbeam.com.

Chapter 7. More Than Smarts and Skill

1. Greg Garber, "A Tormented Soul," An ESPN.com five-part series exploring the life and death of Steelers great Mike Webster, January 24, 2005, http://sports.espn.go.com/nfl/news/story?id=1972285.
2. Ibid.
3. http://www.planetsteelers.com/tag/mike-webster/.
4. Alan Schwarz, "New Sign of Brain Damage in NFL," *New York Times*, January 27, 2009.
5. Caleb Daniloff, "NFL, U.S. Soccer Athletes Donate Brains to BU," *BU Today*, December 22, 2008.
6. Alan Schwarz, "Expert Ties Ex-Player's Suicide to Brain Damage," *New York Times*, January 18, 2007.
7. Jerry DiPaola, "Strzelczyk Killed in Fiery Crash," *Pittsburgh Tribune-Review*, October 1, 2004.

8. Jack Kelly, "Chuck Noll Sparked Concussion Test," *Pittsburgh Post-Gazette*, December 3, 2009.

Chapter 8. Finding Your Life's Work

1. As quoted in Dale Carnegie's classic book, *How to Win Friends and Influence People* (New York: Pocket Books, 1998).

About the Authors

MERRIL HOGE is a former professional football player. He played eight seasons at running back for the NFL's Pittsburgh Steelers and Chicago Bears, and is currently a sportscaster for ESPN television. Merril has fought and beaten cancer, and the thing he cherishes most is being a father.

BRENT COLE has ghostwritten or collaborated on more than thirty books, including seven bestsellers. He is the founder of the Invisible Ink Firm (www.invisibleinkfirm .com), located in Athens, Georgia, where he resides with his wife and two children.